ANXIETY
Insights

What Gets to Us and What Gets Us Through

Lori Maney Lentini

with Nicole Lentini

little pink press™

Published by Little Pink Press, P.O. Box 847, Beacon, NY 12508

ISBN-13: 978-1-7329494-5-4

Dedication

This book is dedicated to all those who deal with anxiety and find the courage each and every day to keep going. You are not alone. As this book is being released amidst the 2020 global coronavirus pandemic, we also dedicate this book to all of the incredible doctors, nurses, medical personnel, military, support, and front-line staff around the world who bravely set aside their fears, anxiety, and concerns for the benefit of others. Thank you all for your sacrifices and courage. You are true heroes.

Disclaimer

The information, methods, and techniques presented in this book are in no way intended to replace appropriate medical and/or psychological treatment. Always consult a qualified and licensed medical and/or mental-health professional before undergoing any treatment for a medical or psychological condition or disorder.

Contents

Acknowledgments

I am truly blessed to be surrounded by loving family and friends who each in their own unique way, love, support, and encourage me to be the happiest, strongest woman I can be every day of my life. I thank all of you.

Any of them could tell you the most important goal in my life is to be a good mom. I am still accepting "perfect" doesn't exist, but I give it my all. My children, Nicole and James are my heart and my life. I want to thank them first for believing in me when I doubt myself. They embraced my goal to write this book as the next step in my journey to eliminate the stigma around mental illness. They bravely participated and offered their stories. Nicole was my initial inspiration and became a contributing author who provided informative and insightful text. James offered daily support, ideas, artwork, and read and edited sections along the way. I am motivated to make the world a better place for them and because of them. I love you both more than you could ever know.

My older sister, Robbie and I could not be more different. This is a blessing as we each bring our own perspective to our relationship and family. She is a college professor and teaches early childhood education. So naturally, she is a grammar- and sentence-structure geek. While in the final months of editing this book, we both moved back to our childhood home to care for our father who was entering the final stage of his life. During this incredibly difficult time, she found the focus, time, and energy to help edit my book. It is a great feeling knowing you can count on family especially when the going gets tough. Thank you Robbie for all your support, both of me as a person and of my professional and advocacy goals.

The saying "You can't make new old friends," has always resonated with me. I want to thank Liz, Robyn, and Traci, whom I have been friends with for almost thirty years. They are among the most compassionate and loyal friends I know. At many points in my life, big or small, happy or sad, healthily or sick, celebrating or grieving, over the years, they have been there. I know they always will be. Naturally, they eagerly volunteered to be interviewed and add their voices to my book. They each have raised a child with mental-health issues and provided insight from a deeply personal place. Each of you hold a special place in my heart and my life. Thank you.

You know when you meet someone, and you immediately get each other. You work well together, and your creativity spurs each other forward. This is my relationship with Rachel, both profession-ally and personally. Over the past year, she has provided me with daily encouragement—I mean, encouragement on steroids. Every day, I would go to her with ideas for this book, for my next book, for social media, and everything technology related. She not only listened but also offered great ideas, edited, and patiently walked me through starting my Facebook, Instagram, and LinkedIn accounts and my website. (Rather, truth be told, she just did it!) Rachel, thank you, and I can't wait to co-author a book with you one day.

This book has been polished to the level we aimed for by Candi Cross, and she worked on it with a sincere passion for the subject matter and improving lives. Thank you, Candi.

Thank you, Keryl Pesce of Little Pink Press who believed in my mission and book. Her goal to facilitate getting stories written by women published to help us live better with less stress and/or suffer-ing was a perfect and successful collaboration. Without her, this book would still just be a document on my computer. Keryl made the pub-lishing process effortless as she brought my book to life and made it available to the world. She is amazing. Thank you.

Finally, to my Worry Warriors: Wendy, Kristen, Breanna, Emily, Jennifer, Zack, Faith, Sam, Jenny, and Jackie—thank you for bravely and selflessly sharing your deeply personal experiences with anxiety to exemplify the message that people living with anxiety and mental illness are not alone. I know it was not an easy decision but was done selflessly with the hope of providing insight into the experience of living with anxiety to help others better understand themselves and those they love who struggle with stress and anxiety. Your contributions and insights are powerful and will make a difference and a dent in the stigma. Thank you for having the courage to raise your voice toward this critical mission.

Preface

Our intention is not to act as clinicians, diagnose anyone with an anxiety disorder, or offer in-depth medical advice on how best to manage anxiety disorders. There are many books (and people more qualified to speak) about how anxiety disorders are defined, diagnosed, and treated. Although we'll use our professional backgrounds to clarify information when necessary, as well as provide explanations and resources as to where to look for more in-depth information, our overarching goal is to share our own and our loved one's deeply personal experiences with anxiety. We want to offer a sense of belonging and community to those who similarly struggle with anxiety or to those who are trying to understand and support a friend, loved one, colleague, student, employee, or neighbor.

Living with a mental illness, including anxiety, is difficult to discuss. It is inherently unsettling to explain something you don't entirely understand about yourself and how your own brain functions. Even if you do find the words to share, there is the worry about being judged, bullied, or seen as inferior or weak. Yet, this isn't the response when you tell someone you have cancer or a heart condition. Anxiety issues are rooted in the biochemistry of our brain and are more difficult to explain than a physical illness. We rarely hear people advocate to power through or just get over physical illness in the same way they judge and tell those with mental illness to just stop worrying.

We believe the best way to effect change is to be bold enough to share our stories and offer information and personal accounts to people both with and without mental illness. We must reinforce that it is simply another medical condition and millions of us are living with it. Just look around, really talk to the people in your life. You will see it too.

Part 1

INTRODUCTIONS: WHAT HAPPENS IN VEGAS
CAN CHANGE YOUR LIFE

Lori: A Book is Born

On a frigid fall Saturday morning before the sun had fully risen, a relentless buzzing penetrated my dream. As my mind slowly emerged from the fog of deep sleep, instinct kicked in, and I rolled over to grab my cell phone from the nightstand. In that split second, my heart skipped a beat, my head started to pound, and I broke out in a cold sweat. Sheer panic shot through my entire body as my thoughts raced. Which of my children was in crisis? Who was hysterical, having a panic attack, in the hospital, or in jail this time? I took a deep breath, fought the now familiar overpowering fear, and answered the phone in what I hoped was my calmest, most reassuring mom voice.

The next few seconds were frozen in time as I assessed her tone and slowly began to exhale; thankfully this wasn't one of those calls. I was certain. From years of experience, I have developed highly accurate internal panic-detection skills when it comes to my children. It was my daughter, Nicole, who was in medical school and unexpectedly struggling. Over the past few months, she noticed a gap starting to grow as her classmates excelled in both personal and academic goals at a dizzying pace. Just watching them was exhausting. They, too, were studying and spending up to twelve hours a day at the hospital, but instead of going home and collapsing, they ran marathons, worked on research projects, and engaged in hobbies, resulting in coverage in national magazines.

Nicole's decision to attend this specific school had been purposeful and part of her life plan. She wanted to challenge herself and ensure she reached her maximum potential. So the logical choice was a highly-ranked and competitive program. She had been at the crossroads of continuing in her comfort zone or stretching and going to a prestigious, acclaimed school. You know, the classic big-fish-little-pond or little-fish-big-pond-life dilemma.

Nicole jumped headfirst into the big pond, a.k.a. Lake Michigan and Northwestern Medicine in Chicago. For the first time in her academic life, she found herself running to keep up instead of winning the race. Then questioning her decision and ability to excel among her highly motivated, intelligent, and talented peers. Was the sacrifice and struggle going to be worth the effort of this self-imposed challenge? If she had chosen to attend a less competitive program, she would still be a doctor when she graduated. Would her choice to take the hard road really ensure her a more successful career? A better life?

As we talked for a while, the conversation gently shifted to how much she loved her program, her advisor, friends, and the city of Chicago. Once she was feeling grounded, she asked how I was doing. We have a close relationship and talk openly about everything. We always have. I count on her for advice, and she offers me new perspectives, often with a healthy dose of honesty. I admitted, more to myself, that I was feeling depressed, sleeping too much, and stuck. *Really stuck.* In my defense, it wasn't like I hadn't done anything. I had thought about "things." Nicole laughed, and said, "Nice try."

She wasn't buying it. We both knew I needed to make changes in my life, but my old friends, Overwhelmed, Stressed, and Anxious, were monopolizing all my energy, focus, and time.

After we hung up, my thoughts drifted back to last December and our girls' weekend in Vegas to celebrate my birthday. Over dinner and a bottle of wine (okay, maybe two), Nicole and I talked about real life; our dreams, fears, and goals. Turning fifty-five had me struggling with where I was in my life and marriage. I was increasingly aware of how dissatisfied I was with what I had done, or perhaps more importantly, not done in my life. I had arrived at the realization that my life was more than half over. My odds of living to be over one hundred seemed like a bad bet. For me, hitting "mid-life" brought with it an unsettling urgency. Telling myself there was plenty of time to pursue happiness or make my mark on the world wasn't working anymore. Because it simply wasn't true. What the hell had I done with fifty years? Seriously, half a century! I had already been alive longer than I had left to live. Quite a sobering thought. Pretty jarring, especially for someone with anxiety issues.

For some bizarre reason, I remembered an art assignment from middle school. The teacher had assigned a project to draw a picture of our tombstone and write our epitaph on it. Pretty weird, perhaps the point was to think about our goals, values, and what kind of person we wanted to be when we grew up. Regardless, I tried to recall what I had written all those years ago. I had no clue. But now, for real, what would it say? *Here lies a beloved mother who died full of good intentions and squandered potential, trapped in an unhappy marriage who never found the guts to pursue her dreams and goals to fulfill her legacy.*

Legacy? What exactly is a legacy? Did I have one? What did I want it to be? Had I accomplished lasting achievements in my life? What had I done to leave the world a better place because I had existed? Was I making a big enough difference in the lives of those around me? What did I care about? What was my biggest regret? Could I fix it? What was my biggest accomplishment? My dream? My passion?

My thoughts were like a game show episode. I knew the question but not the answer. I was coming up empty. I felt like I was about to lose it all.

That night in Vegas over dinner, I had more of these same soul-searching, racing thoughts. Yet, before dessert had arrived and we finished our wine, I knew. Undeniable clarity had set in. I wanted a divorce and I wanted to write my book. I shared this with my daughter.

Nicole was not surprised by the divorce goal. After all, she sat in a front-row seat her entire life as her father and I struggled to be in a functional marriage. We had some good times and supported each other through some tough times, but we mostly failed. She knew I had been unhappy and struggling in our marriage since she was in high school. From my perspective, my ex-husband assumed the role of victim which left me with the responsibility of supporting our family while he was busy pointing out my faults, and I was busy overlooking his. The toxicity level was high for both of us, and I was physically and mentally drained.

On the other hand, my declaration about writing a book was something new. Growing up, she watched as I advocated for mental-health equality, access, and treatment while working for a nonprofit mental-health agency. She was aware I had personal and professional insight into living with stress, anxiety, and mental illness.

Nicole looked at me for a long minute, smiled, and said, "I can see that." She didn't laugh or ask if I was joking. I hadn't yet told anyone I wanted to write a book. It felt beyond me and like a risk; something I could easily fail at doing.

Nicole was interested, so we talked more about my vision of a world where mental illness is accepted and treated like any other illness. One where people are supported, encouraged, and educated to live without shame or under the burden of a stigma because their brain happens to be the organ in their body in need of treatment. Nicole agreed, sharing my journey and experience could inform, support, connect, and help other people. Nicole agreed so much that she offered to be a contributor to the book. We would be a mother-daughter team.

Let's face it: If you are human, stress is part of your life, and there are things that scare you. Maybe your fear is as fleeting as public speaking or heights or snakes, and you can pretty much avoid these situations and things. Or maybe it is as life altering as a fear of leaving your house or dying. Maybe it is a fear of catching the coronavirus. Maybe it is a fear you will live your life alone. Maybe it is a fear your mother will die. Maybe it is a fear everyone in your life actually hates you. Maybe it is a fear you will be in a car accident. Maybe it is a fear you will be kidnapped.

One in four of us will experience a mental health or emotional issue in our lifetime requiring treatment. That is 25 percent of us. That's a whole lot of people, many of whom are hiding their pain. Because society tells them to be ashamed, accuses them of being weak or less than, or tells them (or at the very least infers) it is their fault. One thing I know with complete certainty is they are not weak. You are not weak. It is not their fault. It is not your fault. They are not alone. You are not alone.

Let me say it again. If you are one of us, or love one of us, you are not alone. Maybe you experienced trauma, abuse, a death, a breakup, a divorce, a disability, a serious illness, a miscarriage, a bankruptcy…or dropped out of college and need short-term support. Maybe you struggle with a lifelong mental illness.

Does it really make a difference what is causing your stress and anxiety? It is your mental health, not a competition. Anxiety is anxiety. If it is affecting the quality of your life and you need relief and help, what right does anyone else have to measure or judge your pain? Although our fears and emotions come in different sizes and varieties, adding shame and blame to any of these difficult life changes, events, or illnesses puts up barriers and prevents some of us from seeking medical care. This hurts us all.

We are on a mission to shatter the painful stigma clinging to mental health in our lifetime. We invite you to join us.

Step out of the shadows and seek the support and treatment you or someone you care about needs. Let's talk about panic attacks, depression, and suicidal thoughts the way we talk about diabetes until it becomes the new "normal." Let's acknowledge stress is real. Let's understand more people are experiencing stress and anxiety than ever before in history. Let's help our employers understand we need mental-health days, not just sick days. Let's understand our children are struggling too. Let's educate and train our school, vocational, and college systems to be better prepared to support the emotional needs of all students.

There have been minimal advances in finding a cure or developing new treatments for mental illness over the past few decades. This isn't good enough. We deserve more. Let's advocate to increase funding for research. We need to find actual cures by bringing attention to the need and the number of people who are impacted by emotional and mental-health issues so more or at least adequate funding gets allocated to research. Let's get vocal so our voices are heard.

Reinforce this message: Living with an emotional or mental-health issue doesn't make you any less deserving of respect or treatment. It does not make you any less capable of living a fulfilled, happy life. Millions of us are doing it. Why not talk about it? Share experiences. Learn from each other. Give and accept compassion. Be there for each other. End the loneliness, isolation, and shame. Showcase our strength and bravery by role modeling and owning our power to define who we are and what we want to accomplish.

As we mentioned, some of us experience stress occasionally while others struggle minute by minute, every day, all day. Yes, each of our journeys is unique and deeply personal, but our need for support is the same. It connects us. The amazing, unexpected, beautiful thing is the more we talk about our mental health, the more we gain insight and create understanding and acceptance…both our own and that of society. The shame and blame fades as awareness grows. By talking about our experiences, our families' experiences, and those of close friends, we gain and give comfort, compassion, enlightenment, and share helpful information. Our stories aren't always pretty, but they are real life. Our real lives. We are who we are…people living with a mental illness. We own it. We accept it. We are proud of who we are and what we are accomplishing.

After my phone call that morning with Nicole, as my thoughts settled, it dawned on me, I was all talk and no action. Change is hard! It can't happen without accepting there will be some loss and the belief you have the strength, bravery, or ability to go for the things you want by diving into the unknown. This can be terrifying. I told my children their entire lives they had what it takes to go after their goals, despite their fears. And they did. It was time to put my money where my mouth was and take my own advice. It is so much easier to give advice than take it, even when it is your own.

So, there it was, exposed in the light of day. No denying it. The time for action had arrived.

First, I needed to leave my husband. I spent years living in self-doubt, afraid to leave even though our marriage had crumbled—and we all knew it. It had smoldered for a long time and finally went up in flames. As I sifted through the ashes, I could find blame, hurt, resentment, and anger. Not much else. No support, encouragement, or respect. I needed to break free, dig deep, and do it.

Then a few weeks later, on a warm October morning, I woke up, and while drinking coffee on the porch, felt peace all around me…a weird sense of calm. My husband was on a week-long fishing trip, and the house was empty. I knew couples' counseling wasn't working. I just couldn't do it anymore. The holidays were coming, and they were always the worst. So, why not today? Today could be the day. And it turned out, it was. I did it. I called work and took a "sick day," packed stuff and put it in storage, and moved in with a friend. I remember sitting in her spare room that night thinking, *wow, so that just happened!* After twenty-nine years of marriage, my new life was about to begin.

As I write this, I know that life-altering decision saved me. But at the time, in the moment, it was traumatic and frightening. My entire life plan changed. First there was doubt, drama, and pain. He filed for divorce as I endured bouts of his endless blame, which wasn't anything new. In the end, I found myself blessed with the very things I had prayed for all those years. I could breathe…I mean really breathe …like take a deep breath again for the first time in a long time. I wasn't walking on eggshells questioning my every move and thought, calculating, and trying not to say or do anything to upset him. I had walked over those jagged eggshells, experienced the pain deeply one last time. The freedom from being in a state of apprehension and constantly criticized for what I had done wrong or was about to do wrong or being told what was wrong with me or my family or my friends or even our children, was truly life changing. I was free to rediscover myself…to be me!

This transformation came at a high price in the short term. I was exhausted, depressed, and struggling. I had really wanted to make our marriage work and tried for what felt like an eternity. Because I held on so long, now I was a middle-aged, about to be a divorced woman struggling to summon the energy to simply get out of bed and go to work. You see, I didn't have a choice; I had to help support my kids, support myself, and pay alimony. It was hard. It was lonely. It was depressing. I felt like something or someone had died.

As life settled down, I found a place to live, and the messy, awful divorce lawyer stuff happened. I became fixated on how uncertain my future had become. I was overwhelmed, drowning in my own negativity and lack of self-confidence. All those years of struggling, followed by the complete failure of our marriage had depleted me emotionally. I went to the doctor, he increased my anxiety medication, and I started seeing a new therapist. On the upside, I was all caught up on Netflix. Sound familiar?

One goal down. Divorce in process.

Check.

Next?

Write a book.

After surviving the divorce process, I thought this one would be a piece of cake. But it wasn't. Where was I supposed to generate the energy or motivation to do that? How does one just write a book? The fear of exposing the details of my life and the fear of failure were stressing me out. The stress was making me unproductive.

But the universe had a message. It was telling me something. There were daily reminders, like a voice whispering, "Write the book." Everywhere I went—the gym, the store, the bar, the board-room, the coffee shop, the break room, the dog park, the nursing home, book club, waiting rooms, work, or around my neighborhood, I found myself in discussions with people. People were feeling stress in their lives or were in emotional distress or battling anxiety or sup-porting a loved one with these painful issues. The topic kept coming up in everyday conversations. It was everywhere. It seemed like no one was escaping it. The more stress and anxiety came up and I shared my struggles, the more others had to share. It helped them. It helped me.

Anxiety is a powerful force. Some days we lose the battle, but then there are those glorious days when we are victorious.

There was no doubt stress and anxiety were topics people con-nect with because it was happening daily. This was further confirmed when panic escalated out of control in February 2020 as a pandemic engulfed our lives and locked us in our houses with our fears and thoughts. The twenty-four hour doom and gloom news media seemed to shout daily death counts from around the world. They fo-cused almost exclusively on the negative. Why, I will never under-stand. Because there were so many people helping each other and supporting each other while social distancing. The doctors, nurses, and direct-care staff were putting themselves at risk to help all of us even without enough or proper protective gear and supplies. I wish there was a news station solely focused on the good occurring in the world, because there certainly is plenty of good in the world.

Back then, my challenge wasn't believing what I had to share was relevant; the challenge remained getting it on paper. I was stuck at the intersection of believing I had the insight and experience to share something valuable and being unable to summon the confi-dence or energy to write it.

One afternoon, I was having lunch with a few friends and

blurted out, "I am going to write a book." Once I said it, it seemed real. Within a week, I had not only mastered the art of casually saying, "I'm writing a book," I had started doing it. I summoned the confidence to call myself an author. The more I wrote, the more I believed I was one. Funny how that works.

I think we can agree that stress and anxiety exist in all our lives. For some of us, it is temporary or situational, and for others, it is a lifelong challenge with varying levels of difficulty. Most of the time, my anxiety colors my life just a bit. It adds a tint of grey to the otherwise white clouds in a harmless-looking sky. Other times, my anxiety darkens the whole sky, creating deep, foreboding shades of grey, jet-black, and everything in between.

In the gene pool lottery of life, my children hit the anxiety jackpot. As they physically grew, their fears, phobias, nerves, insecurities, outbursts, and daily anxieties also grew. I was well aware my daughter was suffering, but I had no clue my son was quietly fighting his own raging battle. I still feel guilty and sad I didn't know or support him more. My daughter's anxiety was so prevalent, it demanded my focus. I spent years looking for answers. Why was she so fearful? Was this normal? Did she get this from me? Did she get it from her father? Could she grow up to be a happy, successful adult? Were we doing something wrong? What the hell was happening?

Despite asking directly and repeatedly about her anxiety to multiple medical providers in the early 2000s, no pediatrician seemed to have an opinion, let alone a diagnosis. They had little to offer. They didn't consider her anxiety a medical issue and never recommended we see a psychiatrist. As Nicole became a preteen, she talked less about her anxieties. It seemed, at least outwardly, she needed less reassurance. Maybe she had outgrown it? Was this the end of a horrible, painful phase? Had it just been some kind of mental growing pain? Was it finally over?

In retrospect, my daughter's physical complaints started around the same time the anxiety appeared to settle down: headaches, stomach problems, fatigue, muscle aches, not being able to sleep for more than an hour or two. We saw doctor after doctor and specialists in New York City. Piles of tests were done, but nothing was physically wrong. After about a year, we got better at managing the physical symptoms and stopped going to doctors looking for a magic cure. Life moved on. We didn't consider the possibility that the odd constellation of physical symptoms was rooted in anxiety until Nicole was in college. Then, her anxiety couldn't be denied as it spiraled out of control. This time, as an adult with a different doctor, the diagnosis of generalized anxiety disorder with panic attacks and likely comorbid major depressive disorder came instantly. Treatment in the form of both medication and therapy followed. The improvement in her anxiety was expected. The improvement in the physical symptoms plaguing her for a decade was a shock to both of us.

Nicole shares her personal insights in the next section, but putting a name to this big, scary, anxiety thing we had been dealing with brought us hope. It gave us the language to talk about what was happening. It gave us strategies to deal with it. Once we knew what IT was, we were able to treat IT just like any other medical condition.

This brings me back to that weekend with my daughter in Vegas. As I was getting ready to board my flight for Vegas, Nicole called from Chicago and said she wasn't getting on her flight. She told me she had a panic attack trying to board the plane. She had taken some medication, was starting to calm down, and had rebooked her flight. She wasn't promising she would be able to get on the next flight, but she was sure as hell going to try.

In the past, both of us would have been confused and alarmed by her sudden inability to get on a plane. She had flown back and forth from our home in New York to college in New Orleans and then medical school in Chicago for years with little issue. This made no sense. In the old days, I would have freaked out and dropped everything to try frantically to get to her in Chicago believing she couldn't handle it. She would have gone to the emergency room, sure she was actually dying, only to be sent home hours later. Then the guilt about messing up the trip would have plagued her for months.

The insight we gained into what was going on (a panic attack), why it was happening (usually stress + bad luck), and how long it would last (probably less than an hour after she has taken medication), as well as the lack of actual medical danger (despite feeling like she was having a heart attack), allowed the situation to play out differently this time. I was still upset and scared for my daughter, but she sounded okay on the phone. An hour later, she did get on the next plane. We met in Vegas and moved forward with our vacation that changed my life and kick-started our book.

Lori: I am Woman, Hear Me Roar

My most relevant experience is I am human. I have complicated emotions, fears, and thoughts. I am a passionate mental-health advocate with lived and shared experience supporting family and friends. I have a certification in Mental Health First Aid and Suicide Prevention: QPR with a combination of education and professional and volunteer experience. In 2019, I was appointed as a Mental Health Peer Representative for our Incident Review Committee at work, and I am a member of the Chamber of Commerce Health and Wellness Committee for our county. Living with anxiety and loving people affected by it gives me insight that can't be taught.

For the past few decades, I have worked for a large mental-health organization as the Senior Vice President of Human Resources and Talent Management. Our agency serves over 15,000 patients a year. During much of this time, I led the Quality Assurance and Incident Review process for our clients in programs supporting people with mental health and developmental disabilities ensuring our services, which include mental-health clinics, provide high-quality, effective, and safe treatment. In the past, I oversaw the quality of our services for 12 years, which included investigations regarding abuse, neglect, suicide attempts, completed suicides, and all circumstances or issues impacting the delivery of our physical and mental-health services to our community in twelve counties.

As a major employer in our area, I have the privilege of supporting, coaching, and engaging our almost 2,000 employees. Our staff includes hundreds of people who are severely disabled for work—meaning, they are limited physically or mentally in one or more of their daily living functions, which impacts their ability to live and work without supports and accommodations as medically documented by a doctor. I am proud of our success in getting good-paying jobs over the years for thousands of people with disabilities in our community who were previously viewed as "unemployable." I lead a culture of acceptance and inclusion by offering benefits, programs, and policies to support the health and wellness of all staff, including programs focused on mental health.

I work with staff to achieve and maintain emotional wellbeing. By engaging in difficult and sometimes uncomfortable conversations with employees, I am able to connect them with professional support and services. The trust we build provides the ability to talk honestly about their needs and struggles with mental health.

After years of being in this role professionally and speaking with friends and family about their own workplace experiences, I have an explanation for why my efforts to cultivate an accommodating work environment have been successful: I have personal experience that gives me insight into living with mental-health issues. I consistently lean into my personal experiences and struggles when I talk with employees about issues such as depression, anxiety, or other unstable home situations affecting their lives and work. It gives me credibility.

Simply having an Employee Assistance Program (EAP) does not create a culture of inclusion or invite employees to reach out for help. It takes more. Much more. In the mental-health field, a person who shares he or she lives with a mental-health condition is referred to as a "peer."

    I have supported peers in my personal and professional life living with all types and severity of mental-health issues. Yet, in executive meetings, my input in relation to mental health is often marginalized by leaders who hold a clinical license. They appear to think being clinically trained provides more value than lived experience. I think *different*, not *more* experience.

    When clinicians talk about mental illness, they understandably tend to think of the crisis situations they see in their day-to-day work. They think of the extremes of experiences of their patients, who are often ill to the point of being chronically disabled. They perhaps unintentionally perpetuate stigma about mental illness when they frame all mental illness in this context of extreme severity…situations that evoke pity. This makes it risky for the rest of us at the table to be open about our struggles, lest we be lumped into that category.

    I sit there thinking, *I don't get it. Can't you see us?* Peers are everywhere. They are my family. They are my friends. They are my neighbors. They are my co-workers. They are us. We don't need sympathy. We need judgment-free workplaces. We need to be treated as equals. We need access to affordable, preventive mental-health care. We need to be treated with the same respect and compassion given to people with physical illnesses.

    The people I know living with mental-health issues are compassionate, fun, successful, and leading productive lives. It is not easy, but we are doing it. We are teachers, doctors, musicians, librarians, actresses, waitresses, caregivers, mothers, fathers, sons, daughters, students, and fitness and business professionals. Anxiety lives within and among all of us. It is simply a part of our lives and who we are.

Nicole: The Doctor is In

For the first twenty years of my life, my anxiety ran the show all the time. No matter what I was physically doing—sitting alone watching TV, with friends at dinner, or running errands around town, half of my attention was devoted to managing my anxiety. Alongside whatever else I was doing, I was internally surveying my immediate environment for threats, both physical and emotional. I always expected the worst to happen. I thought this was normal. Constant vigilance was necessary and part of life.

I was not oblivious to the fact that there was something different about me. I was well aware there were things that were harder for me than other people. As a kid, I knew my fears of sleepovers and going on vacation with a friend's family were weird. As a teen, I shared my peers' curiosity of sex, drugs, and alcohol, but those also sounded dangerous and kind of scary, so I was generally happy to let everyone believe I had strict parents. This seemed like a better option than the truth. I was frightened. While I understood the whole fear thing was a bigger problem for me than my friends, I only had half the picture.

I assumed everyone else had the same constant scary thoughts and racing heart that I did, but they just *got over it somehow* and did things anyway.

In college, my anxiety problems finally announced themselves clearly in a series of emergency room visits for what turned out to be panic attacks. After a few months of medication and therapy, it was like a light went on. Everyone around me hadn't been flawlessly jumping over obstacles I had stumbled over my entire life; the obstacles being in my path at all was the abnormal part…not my inability to logic myself over them. When my well-intentioned friends, family, or teachers over the years had tried to empathize with me and share they had anxiety about things, too, but managed to overcome it with a deep breath and positive thinking, *we were talking about entirely different things.*

They (for the most part) had normal day-to-day experiences of the emotion of anxiety. There was an event or situation, like giving a speech in front of the class or talking to the hot guy they were nervous about. It passed, and they moved on with their day. *That* is what everyone thought I was talking about when I mentioned being anxious. After a few months of my anxiety being under more control, I suddenly understood the responses I received whenever I tried to talk about this in the past. People weren't intending to be dismissive by not understanding the severity of what I was experiencing—they simply had no real frame of reference for what I was talking about. I hadn't been able to convey the difference to them since I didn't yet understand it myself.

By the time I started medical school, my anxiety was managed to the point where I only noticed it in some aspects of my day-to-day life. It was no longer controlling me. Now I had an understanding of what my life looked like when my anxiety was under control, so it was easier to notice when it was escalating. I was able to go to the doctor before it got out of control. They could change my medications and prevent full-blown panic attacks. While I was incredibly grateful to the mental-health providers who helped me, I never considered going into psychiatry myself until late in medical school.

In the third year of medical school, you start spending essentially all day, every day, seeing patients (with supervision) either in the hospital or in outpatient clinics, depending on the day. After about eight months of this (including a month early on focused entirely on psychiatry), I noticed the patients I enjoyed working with and/or felt like I had helped the most had some degree of mental illness complicating both their day-to-day lives as well as their management of and ability to cope with their other medical conditions. As I spent more and more time working alongside psychiatrists in different roles and various patient populations, it became increasingly clear to me that I was going to join their ranks. I am currently a resident physician in psychiatry.

My anxiety problems were an isolating experience for most of my life. In the few years that I've been open about my struggles, I've had friends confide in me they were struggling with something similar, and they didn't feel comfortable talking about it until I did. But even among my colleagues who are physicians, when the conversation turns to mental-health issues, it doesn't always seem like they entirely *get it*.

I am as open as I can be in my personal and professional life about my struggles with anxiety (and depression) in an attempt to lessen the stigma and change the reality that even well-trained medical providers are often not clear as to what mental health looks like. I can do more. By adding my story to this collection, as well as helping to compile and medically contextualize the original and compelling stories you'll read about from our family and friends, I am intent on changing the perception of how people view mental illness by providing the insight I have gained as someone on both the patient and provider side of mental healthcare.

Alongside the memoirs in this book, you will find information about anxiety and mental healthcare, as well as some deeper dives in a few areas. Although my medical background helped with putting this information together, my intent in including this is not to act as a doctor or provide specific treatment advice, but to simply provide information on anxiety disorders and treatment options. As you will discover throughout this book, *Anxiety Insights*, an understanding of what's going on in your brain and what you can do about it, is one of the most valuable tools available to cope with living with an anxiety disorder. This is the clarity and understanding to we hope to offer you.

Nicole: Let me Introduce You to my Friend, Anxiety

To those affected, anxiety can strike often, unexpectedly, and at the most inconvenient of times. It tags along, uninvited, to work, school, the store, the gym, or even on a date. Anxiety can make our thoughts feel jumbled and our minds feel crowded. We can live our daily lives in a state of anxious overdrive that causes constant physical exhaustion or even pain from unconsciously tensing muscles for hours at a time. Looping, repetitive thoughts take up mental processing power and limit our ability to concentrate. The more unhealthy thoughts repeat, the more ingrained they become in our minds, giving them strength. Anxiety prevents us from sleeping. It makes us irritable and places our temper on edge. It creates a pervasive sense of concern about future threats and failures, inhibiting our ability to relax or de-stress, even when we have the time.

Anxiety convinces us everyone is watching, judging, and disapproving. It gets in the way of our ability to maintain relationships. It causes us to take seemingly illogical actions or makes us appear flaky or uncaring. We struggle to explain why we're cancelling plans we were enthusiastic about hours ago when nothing has outwardly changed. The truth is much has changed, but it is locked in our minds. Sometimes anxiety prevents us from returning phone calls in the first place. When we think about reaching for the phone, our anxiety reflexively reminds us we may say or do something wrong and embarrass ourselves or upset someone. So, we just give up altogether. We fear having a panic attack in public and despite wanting to socialize, we choose to stay home instead. As our anxiety increases, we often find ourselves "busy."

We are, in fact, busy. Busy battling overwhelming or self-loathing thoughts. We're busy trying to keep our heads above water or busy being too exhausted to do anything but go to bed and be alone where we don't have to pretend to be okay. Most of all, we're busy trying to come up with a way to explain this to friends and family in a way that makes any sense…an explanation that sounds better than "I just can't do that today," or, "I would love to be there, but I cannot get out of bed today."

Living with any mental illness (including anxiety) is isolating and intimidating to discuss. It's inherently unsettling to attempt to explain something you don't entirely understand about yourself. Even when we know what we want to say, we may worry about the downstream effects of opening up about anxiety such as being judged, bullied, or seen as inferior or weak.

On some level, we understand our fears can be illogical, unlikely, and out of proportion. Knowing this doesn't change the fear's grip over us, nor does it mean we can push the fear aside and move on with our day. This paradox is as frustrating to us as it is to our well-intentioned loved ones trying to talk us out of our anxiety.

Maybe your experiences with fear and anxiety are infrequent and manageable. Maybe you're secretly terrified of small spaces or clowns but have managed to structure your life in a way this rarely causes you problems. Most of us are afraid of things like public speaking, crowds, heights, elevators, germs, spiders, or snakes on some level. The bigger question is: Have your fears reached the point where they consume most of your thoughts or exert control over almost every area of your life?

Mental illnesses, including anxiety, are invisible conditions, making them difficult to understand from the outside or explain from the inside. The forthcoming narratives are all personal stories centered around the experience of living with an anxiety disorder. We share these stories (our own and those contributed by friends and family) to increase understanding and decrease stigma related to living with mental illness. It was not an easy decision for either of us or our contributors to share our stories openly. We did so with the hope of providing insight into the experience of living with anxiety, to help you better understand yourself or those in your personal or professional life who are struggling or may struggle in the future.

For most of us, the battle with anxiety will be life long. Our individual experiences with managing stress and anxiety vary incredibly in how they manifest, when they started, and the ways we treat them. Throughout the book, we have not altered the facts. Each of us is at a different point in our journey. Some of us have been successfully treated. Some haven't chosen treatment…yet. Some are in treatment. Many others are somewhere in between. There is no right or wrong way to have anxiety.

If this sounds familiar, we hope you'll find solidarity in numbers and that hearing stories of other people who successfully live with anxiety will offer encouragement. We hope you find our stories individually and collectively hopeful, informative, inspiring, and comforting. Our vivid and honest accounts of how we endure and thrive are offered to help you and those in your life. If you've never struggled with pathological anxiety, we hope to give you a backstage glimpse into what everyday life is like for someone living with severe anxiety.

My mom and I spent years misunderstanding and miscommunicating the differences in our own experiences with stress, anxiety, and fear. We internalized our daily struggles with anxiety as personal failings to handle normal life problems (or solve our children's problems) rather than signs of a medical condition.

Although rooted in the biochemistry of our brains, mental illnesses are almost always more difficult for others to understand and empathize with than physical illnesses. They are, in many ways, invisible. We rarely hear people advocate to power through or get over physical illness in the ways people seem to do with mental illness. People don't question the realness of physical limitations in the ways that are fair game for mental illnesses.

Whether you are a parent, child, spouse, family member, friend, care provider, mentor, teacher, volunteer, or professional, we hope you gain insight about yourself, those you love, support, educate, or treat.

Brief Facts About Anxiety Disorders

Although the experience of anxiety in our day-to-day lives is too personal to be easily defined or categorized into boxes, ironically, the easiest way to start a conversation about anxiety is to both clarify definitions and define the types of anxiety.

Understanding the basics of clinical anxiety disorders can help develop insight that assists in understanding both our loved ones and ourselves.

The memoirs of our family and friends that follow are the real-life genuine accounts of courage, grit, and resilience, with a dash of humor. Feel free to read straight through this section as an introduction or jump to the stories first and use this section as a reference later—it works either way! The integration of both the science and lived experiences is what we are going for here as we embark on deepening insight.

Anxiety vs. Anxiety Disorders

Anxiety is, in the simplest terms, the fear of something happening in the future. Although there are endless ways to classify anxiety, let's start with two main types of anxiety: *normal anxiety* and *pathological anxiety*.

When we refer to *normal anxiety,* we mean the emotion everyone experiences from time to time in their daily lives. This anxiety can be annoying. It can cause our mind to go blank and make us lose our place in the middle of an important presentation. It can cause our hands to shake just enough to betray our efforts to not show how nervous we are at the beginning of an interview. This is the type of anxiety that is well represented not only in our daily experiences, but also, throughout the media. Being so nervous you drop the ring in the middle of a proposal or the kid who comes downstairs on the first day of school with his shirt on backwards are both examples of people experiencing *normal anxiety.*

It's not all bad. Some stress is a part of life and is healthy and often helpful. Stress related to deadlines motivates us to finish projects. The stress of keeping our jobs and paying bills gets us to work on the days when we'd rather sleep in. In many performance situations, people perform better under the stress of being watched by others. Similarly, we all experience *normal anxiety*, maybe even intense anxiety from time to time, but usually, it's limited to particular situations or it is infrequent enough it doesn't impact our day-to-day lives or choices. This is the anxiety that it's possible (and maybe even healthy) to *just push through.*

Our stories and those of the people you'll hear from in the coming narratives are people who have spent large portions of their lives living with the other kind of anxiety: *pathological anxiety.* The line between *normal anxiety* and *pathological anxiety* is fuzzy and sometimes hard to identify, even for medical professionals. Basically, *pathological anxiety* is day-to-day anxiety's steroid-taking, jacked-up bully of a twin sibling.

When the degree and intensity of anxiety (or any mental-health disorder) becomes severe enough to interfere with multiple areas of our lives and directly cause us problems with our relationships or our careers, or forces us to make changes to our regular behaviors or routines, it probably meets criteria to be referred to as a "disorder." There's a phrase the *DSM* (basically the bible of psychiatry) uses as a key criterion to diagnose any mental illness: "…causes clinically significant distress or impairment in social, occupational, or other important areas of functioning."[1]

What is "clinically significant distress or impairment?" That's a slightly different question and one without exact objective criteria. This, combined with the fact that some level of anxiety is a normal human experience, leads to an understandable level of the disconnect in people's ability to acknowledge and understand what having a true anxiety disorder feels like from the outside.

Considering everyone experiences and manages a degree of anxiety, it can be hard to recognize when anxiety is severe enough to be causing significant problems in someone's life. These disorders tend to start slowly and escalate over time if untreated, making it more difficult for people to maintain normal insight into when their behaviors have crossed the line requiring professional help. Even worse, since we all live with some amount of anxiety, when we see someone we know with anxiety that is causing them real problems, we tend to say (or at least quietly believe) the reason they are having issues is that they "aren't strong enough to deal with it" or "are too high-strung" or "need to learn how to relax" or any iteration of that sentiment.

People who suffer from anxiety can internalize this and begin to believe it themselves, preventing them from recognizing their anxiety as a medical issue or asking their doctor for advice.

Just like everyone's fingerprints are different, everyone's brain is different. Some of us are not going to be able to "calm down" or "learn to relax" without help. Even the same person at different points in life may be able to manage his anxiety and keep it from overpowering him and at other times, needs help.

Here's a reference sheet of things that fall into "clinically significant distress or impairment" or what we're calling *pathological anxiety*. This is not an absolute or all-inclusive list. It can be helpful to see the kinds of criteria mental-health professionals look at when evaluating "function." Everyone has bad days or things they feel particularly anxious about, but as a general frame of reference, your anxiety should not regularly be stronger than:

- Your ability to attend school or work
- Your ability to get rid of things you no longer need
- Your ability to form and maintain relationships
- Your ability to control your worries about how relatively minor pains or sensations may mean imminent medical doom and landing you in the ER
- Your ability to leave the house without double- or triple-checking the locks. Or the candles. Or the curling iron
- Your ability to leave the house
- Your ability to obtain the things you need: groceries, medical care, employment
- Your ability to focus on day-to-day tasks
- Your ability to get through your day without having panic attacks
- Your ability to tolerate change or uncertainty

The main point is: If people have anxiety at a level that is impacting their lives in negative ways on a day-to-day basis, they likely need help. There's nothing wrong with that. There is also not a single definition of "help." The type of help people need depends on the specific conditions under the umbrella of "anxiety" they are feeling, what their brain chemistry is like, their family history of mental illness, the areas of their life impacted, and what their personal goals are in terms of controlling their anxiety.

Some people benefit from brief support, while others find great results with *cognitive behavioral therapy* (basically retraining the neural networks in your brain—cool stuff), some people need medication. Some people need all of the above.

Needing help for mental health isn't a personality defect or a weakness. It isn't any different than seeing a doctor because you broke your arm, and you need it casted. You technically could do that yourself, I guess. But would you? You likely don't know much about bones or casts, so assuming you're lucky enough to have access to healthcare, why would you struggle through trying to treat yourself? Mental illness is no different. Countless professionals have experience and expertise in treating illnesses of the mind. Let them help. Please don't judge others for needing help. Please don't tolerate others judging you, and certainly, don't judge yourself.

Global Burden of Anxiety Disorders
So far, we've talked about how anxiety is an emotion everyone experiences which can, under certain circumstances, progress from an occasional emotion to a distressing disorder. But how common is it for this progression to become a true disorder that needs treatment? How much trouble can it cause people, and what can treatment do?

In terms of being common, anxiety disorders are the most common mental-health condition in both adults and children worldwide. The current global prevalence rate for anxiety disorders is 7.3%, meaning that one in every fourteen people around the world meets the criteria for an anxiety disorder at any given time.[2] This number rises to one in nine if instead of looking at a specific point in time, we look at the number of people who will experience an anxiety disorder in any given year.[3] I'll repeat that one. *One out of every nine people around the world will struggle with a significant anxiety disorder every year.* Focusing on the United States alone, 18% of adults will struggle with an anxiety disorder in any given year and over a lifetime, almost 30% of adults will at some point in their life, meet criteria for an anxiety disorder.[2] That's a lot of people.

As will become a major theme across this book, anxiety isn't a disorder limited to adults. In fact, most anxiety disorders begin in childhood or adolescence. A recent nationwide survey found that 31.9% of teenagers will experience an anxiety disorder with some degree of clinical impairment before age 18 (8% will experience an anxiety disorder considered to be severely impairing).[4] Although the overall rates of anxiety disorders do decrease with age, anxiety isn't limited to younger people, and it isn't a normal phase that teenagers or young adults experience and then simply just outgrow.

In one study specifically examining the course of anxiety disorders, 50% of boys who had an adolescent anxiety disorder had at least one more episode in young adulthood. For girls, the rate was even higher at 65%.[5] So, if it happens in middle school or high school, chances are it might happen again later in life. But even for the lucky people who do learn to cope with their anxiety and "grow out of" meeting criteria for an anxiety disorder as they get older, the effects of coping with anxiety disorders during adolescence (especially when undertreated) lasts into adulthood. Childhood and adolescent anxiety disorders are associated with later development of further anxiety disorders, depression, substance use, as well as educational underachievement, early parenthood,[4] and lower workforce participation and income as an adult .[5] There are concrete benefits to treating anxiety disorders quickly and effectively rather than trying to "tough them out," "get over it," or "just deal with it."

The long-term outcomes don't support the idea of "what doesn't kill you makes you stronger" when it comes to mental-health disorders. The data, in fact, generally supports the complete opposite: *Mental illness does the least long-term harm to an individual when it is recognized, diagnosed, and effectively treated as quickly as possible.* I've worked with many patients who think taking medication for mental illness makes them weak or prevents them from developing coping skills in some way. It doesn't. Although this is true for most mental illnesses, it is especially true for anxiety disorders. Medications often help temper down the excess of alarm bells going off inside someone's mind to help them think clearly enough to focus on coping skills or solving larger problems—that's the therapy part.

So, how bad is the problem? Psychiatric disorders and substance use are currently the number one cause of disability worldwide. [6] Although it's tempting to dismiss this number as artificially inflated by those suffering from psychotic disorders such as schizophrenia who have overall low levels of workforce participation, that's not really the case here.

While it's true that our cultural stereotype is that "mentally ill people" (generally people suffering from severe psychotic disorders and homelessness) struggle to maintain employment or housing without assistance, by the numbers, there just aren't that many people suffering from psychotic illnesses. Rates of psychotic illness are fairly stable worldwide and hover in the range of 1-2 % of the population. But mental illness is the number one cause of disability worldwide—more than back pain, more than cancer, and more than workplace accidents.

Where are the rest of the "severely mentally ill?" Typically, suffering as quietly as possible to avoid that "mentally ill" label being applied to themselves.

Looking at just anxiety disorders, when compared with *both* physical and medical disabilities, anxiety disorders are still overall, the sixth leading cause of disability in both high-and low-income countries.[2] Anxiety and it's very close friend, depression, account for 55% of all disability-adjusted life years attributable to mental disorders.[7] Again, people often find these numbers surprising because they don't think that they personally know anyone struggling with such a severe mental-health condition that they can't consistently work, but they likely do. They just don't know it.

Particularly devastating from a population level, anxiety disorders (and some other mental-health conditions) are particularly nasty because they tend to most commonly and most severely affect younger people. The highest burden of anxiety disorders globally is from ages 15-34.[2] The problem with people being significantly less productive or taking them out of the workforce entirely due to anxiety disorders at this crucial time in their lives, is that the disruption is happening at a particularly vulnerable time when many people are trying to finish school or start careers. This may have long-term effects like delaying (or even preventing) graduations or causing early career failures that require years to recover from.

Looking only at young adults, psychiatric disorders and substance abuse account for 45% of total disability in this age group.[6] Overall, the estimate is that anxiety disorders cost the United States alone more than $42 billion a year.[8]

Many studies focus on workforce participation and disability days because they are relatively easy-to-measure metrics that objectively measure the degree of distress and impairment a disorder is causing in day-to-day functioning. This is not the only metric by which anxiety disorders have been found to be significantly disabling. The same years are also crucial for establishing social connections and long-term relationships. For example, social anxiety, in particular, in addition to detriments in school and work performance, has been associated with affected individuals having impaired social relationships, fewer friends, and being less likely to date or marry than those without social anxiety disorder.[8] Finally, anxiety disorders (and mental-health conditions, in general) dramatically increase the chances that an individual will develop a substance use disorder (a problem with alcohol or drugs).[4]

It's not all doom and gloom; reduction in symptoms achieved through medication and/or therapy yields meaningful improvement in both disability metrics and overall quality of life.[2] It's not an unfixable problem, and there are things that can be done to help. And not surprising, the most important (and often most difficult) step in getting help is correctly identifying the problem. That's where professionals can generally step in and help.

Nicole: Insight and Stigma:

Did You Say Help?

Who Needs Help?

I spent my first six months of medical residency working as a medical intern (with the doctor title, for the first time!) in the general medicine, emergency, pediatrics, and neurology departments of the hospital. This was an especially interesting experience for me because while I was functioning as a full-time member of the service and working alongside my medicine colleagues doing all the same things and seeing all the same patients for the months I was there, I never really stopped being an undercover psych intern.

Given my history of seeing probably close to 50 doctors with nonspecific physical complaints as a child/early teen and never getting any real answers or guidance on what to do next (even though many of the doctors clearly thought this "wasn't physical"), I was primed to notice similar behavior from the healthcare provider side in other people. It didn't seem uncommon for a medicine or emergency team to do all the appropriate testing, ask the right questions, and ultimately very clearly identify a patient's particular complaint as primarily a psychiatric (usually anxiety) issue without ever actually connecting the patient to psychiatric resources. This also seemed unique to psychiatry. Patients with heart or brain problems not serious enough for inpatient admission usually left the emergency room (ER) with referrals to follow up with a cardiologist or neurologist, as was appropriate. Psychiatry referrals were less common. Why? The first reason is well known to anyone who has ever personally tried to navigate the mental healthcare system: There aren't enough resources, and wait times are months to years long. The second reason, lack of insight, is both more complicated and, in my experience, more common.

I had observed similar interactions of anxiety disorders from the provider side during medical school. Most commonly, it goes something like this: Someone comes into the ER with a collection of odd symptoms that don't immediately fit into any clear medical condition. The ER team does their due diligence, runs tests, ensures the patients are medically stable (not at risk of dying if they go home), attributes their ER visit to "anxiety" and send the patients home. What they rarely do is talk at all to the patients about their anxiety, how often these ER visits are happening, or what can be done to help them manage the anxiety after they go home.

My intern year of experience in these situations outside of the psychiatry department gave me the chance to be the one in the emergency department, acting as the ER doctor, telling people we had run all the tests and based on the results, their very scary symptoms appeared to be secondary to their intense anxiety, and trying to talk about the next steps.

I was always careful with how I phrased things. I was careful to avoid the traps I had seen other doctors fall into. I emphasized the physical symptoms and experiences as real and explained they weren't signs of something life threatening (like a heart attack). I never referred to it as "just anxiety." I never presented anxiety as the "since we couldn't find anything else wrong with you… I think it's in your head" type diagnosis. I was as clear, empathetic, and reassuring as I could be: "The symptoms are very real, and I believe everything you've told me about your symptoms."

I would go on to say, "Your symptoms are consistent with an anxiety disorder which can, by itself cause a lot of these physical symptoms or make existing physical symptoms flare up. It's something we see often. The good news is we're able to say with 100% confidence that your heart is fine, and there are really great treatment options available for your anxiety. Sometimes there's a bit of a wait to get in, but I have names of doctors who take your insurance and are taking new patients. I'm also happy to talk to your primary care provider, who may be able to start treatment in the meantime while you're waiting to see a psychiatrist (who I always made sure to separately explain, is a medical doctor, no couches or hours-long discussions about your childhood necessarily need to be involved)."

Call it naivety, but I had seen numerous conversations like this handled poorly by doctors while I was still a student. I honestly thought if I did it better, I could help patients understand. In reality, although some people were in a place where they were able to hear and accept that diagnosis, I mostly got yelled at…a lot. About half of the patients were "never going to go talk to any goddamn shrink" and were off to find "another emergency room that knows what they're doing" or "someone who actually believes me" before I could even finish my first sentence. Another portion didn't yell, but basically took the papers, rolled their eyes, and left without another word. This echoed what several internal medicine and emergency medicine doctors told me when I had questioned why they didn't share the depths of their concerns about how out of control the patient's anxiety was getting (fourth ER visit this month kind of stuff)—patients don't want to hear it. They struggled to accept it.

As the psych intern, it was a uniquely fascinating and demoralizing experience. These weren't patients I would get the chance to see as a psychiatrist. They were self-selecting themselves out of our pool of patients long before they ever crossed the threshold into our office. We would get consulted and asked to talk to some of them in the hospital when the inpatient medical team was concerned, sure. But they still self-selected out pretty quickly; they almost always threw us out of their rooms as soon as we introduced ourselves. It's not like you can force someone to talk to you, even if you are the doctor. While acting "undercover," I had already spent hours talking to these patients. I knew them, to some extent. I had heard their whole story of the past months to years of ongoing medical issues. And the part that slowly ate away at my soul was that I knew that psychiatry could help them, if they would just let us.

The reason it is such a challenging conversation to have from the medical provider side and that it feels like a devastating diagnosis for many patients to accept is multipronged. There are complex reasons influenced by hundreds of different things from how you were raised and your cultural beliefs to your prior experiences with the medical system. I would like to use this relatively common experience that I believe most people with anxiety can relate to in order to talk about two related concepts which are central to discussions throughout this book: Insight and Stigma.

Insight

Insight is a word we use quite often throughout the book. In a strict dictionary context, insight is "a deep understanding of a person or a thing." In psychiatry, insight is a slightly more loaded word that specifically refers to someone's awareness of their own problematic behaviors and an understanding of the causes of those behaviors. Insight is usually closely tied to motivation to change (or accept treatment).

To expand upon the example we were talking about earlier, think about a patient who comes to the emergency room for the third time in a year with chest tightness and shortness of breath who, after ruling out scary things, is determined to have symptoms related to anxiety. I will not pretend doctors are perfect and never misdiagnose things, but let's go with his or her symptoms are 100% due to anxiety for the sake of this example.

This generally goes one of three ways.

One. Patients say something like, "I'm pretty sure this is related to my anxiety, but *it is chest pain,* and it's kind of freaking me out, so I came here to make sure that it's not my heart." That's a pretty good level of insight. These people may still need help in getting their anxiety controlled to the point where it isn't causing them to be physically uncomfortable and scared to the point where hospital visits once a month seem reasonable. But overall, chances are good they'll accept it when the doctors say they agree it is anxiety and recommend the patients see their regular doctor and maybe a psychiatrist about their increasingly hard-to-control anxiety. These patients generally do well long-term. They're often aware the main concern bringing them into the ER is anxiety, and they're open to treatments to help them control the anxiety. They usually seek treatment in an outpatient psychiatry clinic.

Two. The second possibility (and my personal favorite outcome) is the patients haven't really considered anxiety as a possible cause of their symptoms, but they are in a place where they're able to listen to the explanation about the kinds of symptoms anxiety can cause, why their symptoms are likely anxiety related, ask follow-up questions, and think about if this "sounds like them." At the end of it, anxiety is an explanation that *makes sense to them,* and they're willing to see psychiatrists, see what they think, and consider trying anxiety treatment, especially since nothing else has worked for them yet. They didn't end up getting the help that they expected when the visit started, but they got the help that they needed.

All's well that ends well.

Three. This is where things get messy and frustrating from all sides. The patients come in with the same symptoms, no idea where they may be coming from other than their heart, and throughout their entire time in the ER, basically continue to demand a physical explanation from their doctors. It's a frustrating interaction from both sides. The patients are convinced something is physically very wrong, and no one is taking them seriously. The doctors are frustrated because these are textbook panic attacks, they've run more testing than they really needed to in order to confirm that nothing else is wrong, and the patients just won't listen to or believe their diagnosis. They could likely help the patients if the patients could *believe them*.

Despite best efforts, trust breaks down, and the patients leave still upset that something is very wrong, often to go to another doctor or hospital who will take them "more seriously" and repeat the entire process over again. Done enough times, sometimes invasive testing is performed to "make sure" nothing is wrong. There can be very concrete harm done in this kind of situation, but more upsetting for me is no amount of reassurance helps the patients feel any better. So throughout this entire process (which can easily go on for months or years)—the patients are still suffering. They believe there is something wrong with their body and actively causing them harm and no doctor can find it or help them. They start to feel hopeless about the future, doubt their ability to cope with their condition "forever," or even like they're trapped in a body that's slowly betraying them. It's incredibly difficult.

The truth is, without some degree of agreement as to what the problem actually is, fixing it is near impossible. And although we can get pictures of the brain itself, there's no way to get a scan or test that "proves" anxiety disorders (as of right now). So even if over the course of 14 ER visits, we scan the entire body, we're still not going to be able to *see*, or *show you*, or *point to* the problem. We can *treat* the problem, but only when the patient is willing to accept the diagnosis, which is where this can get tricky.

Psychiatry often falls into a rare category of medical diagnosis that, from the patient perspective, seems like we're asking for you to

accept our opinion on faith. Although psychiatry is a medical disci-
pline grounded in decades of research, psychiatric diagnoses (particularly when people were seeking general medical care) often feel
subjective when there's no equivalent of an x-ray with a clearly broken bone or an abhorrent lab value to point to that justifies their
conclusion like people typically expect from their physicians. Also,
while there are many effective treatments for anxiety disorders, there
is no magic pill for anxiety disorders. All of the treatments take time,
commitment, and a desire to change. This combination of not feeling
sure of a diagnosis they can't see and not liking the treatments that
are being offered for it, tempts people to continue to seek another
explanation.

I remember this conversation when I was the patient. I had seen
doctors with nonspecific complaints for years (muscle aches, heart
palpitations, etc.), and no one had been able to explain the origin of
any of my symptoms. At the time, my anxiety had progressed to the
point I was having panic attacks and going to the ER. One of these
times I had again come to the hospital thinking something was physically very wrong with me. But by the end of the doctor's less than
five-minute explanation about anxiety disorders (including the things
like muscle aches that had been bothering me for years), his explanation just made complete sense to me. I knew I was more anxious
than other people, even if I thought that I managed it okay. I was
familiar with the symptoms he mentioned. The whole thing made
sense, and I thought it might explain the problems I'd been having. I
took his referral, saw a psychiatrist a week later, had a detailed conversation about my symptoms over the years and was given a longer
and more in-depth explanation about anxiety disorders, which resonated with me. I started taking medication that day and going to therapy within a few weeks. It went well. The anxiety was treated, and I
felt better. By that point, I had been suffering from a severe anxiety
disorder that had gone unrecognized and untreated for somewhere in
the range of 12 to 14 years.

Many of the stories you'll hear throughout this book are, at their core, about the ways people came to terms with their anxiety, the ways it was affecting their lives, and what they did to control it, a.k.a. their personal journeys to gaining insight into their own condition that allowed them to take actions to limit anxiety's grip on their lives. For me, the understanding step was the hardest step in controlling my anxiety. I spent years not understanding the problem. Once I did, the medication, therapy, and the where-do-we-go-from-here steps came easily. For others, the path was a little bit different.

Why is it so hard to 1) find a doctor who correctly identifies the anxiety as a problem needing to be treated; 2) find a doctor who explains anxiety disorders to a patient in a way they can understand; 3) have a patient accept anxiety as a potential cause for their symptoms; and 4) get someone into anxiety-focused treatment? Numerous reasons. And although I'm admittedly biased given my undergraduate area of research in social psychology and specifically, stigma, I think it is worth discussing the very prevalent individual and collective stigmas about mental health and mental-health conditions that affect how people think about mental health long before they ever see a doctor. Stigma is responsible for most of the stark differences in how patients respond to psychiatry diagnoses and every other medical diagnosis and remains a monumental barrier to both insight and treatment for many people.

Stigma

Stigma is a prejudice, based on stereotypes, that results in discrimination.[9] Stay with me. Basically, people who are stigmatized have some quality about them that causes them to be seen as different and lesser in the eyes of others. This can be gender, race, sexual orientation, nationality, immigration status, physical deformities, disability, or socioeconomic status.[9] Stigma can exist for almost any group membership. Stigma, at its core, sets up a system of insiders and outsiders. It breaks people down to *us* vs. *them*.

Although the idea that people are treated unfairly or poorly by society as a whole due to any of these (largely unchangeable) group memberships is, by itself, upsetting—that isn't the only problem. Stigma doesn't only affect how other people view members of a stigmatized group; it also affects how members of that group view themselves. And especially in terms of mental health, stigma against those with mental illness can become a huge barrier in people's willingness to seek help.[10]

We understand the world around us, in many ways, through other people. As young children, we internalize the things that our parents or caregivers tell us as "the truth" because it's all we know. As we get older, spend more time with peers, meet new people, and expand our worldview, we start to get the information that forms our overall perspectives from more varied sources. But the most basic way that we learn what is socially acceptable and what is not is from observing the words and actions of those around us, especially the people with whom we spend a lot of our time or those we admire. In our currently interconnected world, these opinions and perspectives are also influenced by the constant barrage of words and images in the media that we choose to consume, all depicting some version of the "real world"—none of them without their own inherent biases and interpretations.

If no one around you ever talks about needing help with their own mental health, and the only times you see discussions of the "mentally ill" are on the news in relation to crimes or mass shootings, dramatized in movies, or in hushed conversations about that cousin that you don't really talk about anymore—the mentally ill become a *them*. If your perception of *them* is limited to "One Flew Over the Cuckoo's Nest," and you don't think you're quite ready to join the cast, you're not going to react well to the suggestion that you see a psychiatrist, no matter how carefully phrased or well intentioned.

What's worse is that for mental health, in particular, stigma also creates a vicious cycle of silence. Even if you do eventually see the shrink, even if he or she helps you, even if you learn that most people who see a psychiatrist do so once every few months on their lunch hour from work and not locked in an institution as prison diversion, you probably won't be going around freely sharing that revelation with most of the people in your life. Why? You won't want people to start seeing you as mentally ill, one of *them*. What's the end result? The people going about their day-to-day lives with mental illness don't talk about it, and the common understanding of what mental illness *is* and *looks like* is limited to scripted dramas, the cable news, third-hand community gossip, or folks struggling so much they're wandering outside talking to themselves and clearly in crisis.

Well, we'll just all start talking openly about our mental illnesses then, you say. Problem solved, right? Sort of. This is the trend, and what people are moving toward over time. But society moves slowly. It's important to keep in mind that the peak of the mass institutionalization era—where families would send relatives with mental illnesses to live indefinitely at large institutions out of sight and stop mentioning them around friends at home lest people would think they were a "bad family"—was in the 1950s and 60s. It's hard to think of a more dramatic example of *us* vs. *them*. Some of the shift since then towards supporting folks with even fairly severe mental illnesses living in the community has to do with improvements in psychiatric medications, but a lot of it has to do with efforts to decrease stigma around mental illness. Although it's a common stereotype of those who suffer from mental illness, "different" doesn't always (or even usually) mean dangerous.

Today, people my age are much more likely to casually start a sentence with "Well my therapist said…." or reference the medication they take for their mood in casual conversation with friends than most people would have even 10 or 20 years ago. We're making progress as a whole, but there's still room to improve.

As much as I hope it won't be the case in the future, right now, people with mental illnesses do still experience significant stigma. On top of the fun of dealing with the stress of your mental illness, the experience of stigma is also, in itself, stressful. In the moment, experiencing stigma can increase anxiety levels, increase blood pressure, increase stress hormones in the body, decrease working memory capacity, and overall trigger "fight or flight" type responses that are rarely appropriate to the situation at hand.[9] These are the kinds of physical fear responses you need to run from a bear, and they're basically useless when you're trying to run from judgment, but your sympathetic nervous system doesn't really know the difference. Over time, when this physical fear response is activated over and over again, this likely contributes to the significantly higher burden of physical illnesses such as hypertension, heart disease, and stroke within people who are stigmatized. Being a member of a stigmatized group has, in general, been linked to poorer outcomes in areas of life other than physical health as well including academic underachievement, poverty, and decreased access to housing, education, and jobs.[9]

Stigma regarding mental illness, specifically, is not a new idea— a lot of research has been done on this topic. Stigmas about different groups all have specific associations for what that group of people is "typically" like. For mental illness in particular, group members are commonly thought of as unpredictable, incompetent, dangerous, or untrustworthy. These are dominant ideas within our culture, and research has shown that by age 10, most children are aware of these specific stereotypes.[9] It's also evident in the language commonly used around mental illness. People *have* heart disease or *have had* a heart attack. People *are* schizophrenic or *are* mentally ill.

Stigma doesn't just affect our lives on an individual level. The trickle-down effects of mental-health stigma are apparent at larger societal levels. First, cultural beliefs about mental health, what mental illness is, and what people who suffer from mental illnesses are like influences the kinds of policies and practices that we enact to address these issues as a society.[11] It influences our shared beliefs about what is likely and what is possible. For example, when policymakers believe (as many people do) that mental illness isn't treatable, they resist efforts to fund mental-health treatment. Similarly, mental healthcare is still reimbursed at a lower rate by most insurance companies (and requires higher out-of-pocket costs for patients) than physical healthcare. This is allowed to continue, in large part, because of stigma against those with mental illness and beliefs such as; mental illness is untreatable, those with mental illnesses won't ever contribute significantly to society, or that mental illness is somehow the fault of (or a weakness of) the individual.

An example given in a review paper on mental health stigma[12] which I think is a powerful illustration of how this kind of process plays out in daily life, is to imagine insurance companies got together tomorrow and said they were only going to cover 50% of any heart-related medical problems. There's an argument to be made that most of the factors contributing to cardiac disease are lifestyle related (smoking, obesity, lack of exercise) and controllable by the individual. Although this is obviously a horrible idea, I could make an argument for it. I could probably make a better argument for excluding heart- or obesity-related conditions (largely lifestyle risk factors that are modifiable) from health insurance policies than I could make to exclude mental-health conditions (largely unmodifiable risk factors like genetics or prior exposure to trauma). But it would never be allowed to happen—people would fight back. They would be appalled. Lawmakers and regulatory agencies would be quick to step in. But even today, we don't yet view mental health as the same as physical health, and it's common for it to be more expensive or limited to get mental healthcare under an insurance policy than it is any other kind of healthcare.

The stigma against mental illness has a few final and surprising ways that it trickles down to harm those in need of mental-health services. Even if individuals are surrounded by extraordinary family and friends and isolated from some of the direct experiences of stigma, it still affects their treatment and care. Psychiatry has not been typically thought of as a prestigious specialty for doctors considering their specialty choices and remains among the lowest-paying medical specialties. This influences which doctors and how many doctors are willing to choose psychiatry as a specialty (although this is also changing among younger medical school graduates), which ultimately determines the eventual availability of and wait time to see providers for patients in need. Additionally, considering psychiatric illnesses are some of the most common illnesses experienced by patients worldwide, coverage of mental-health research in major academic journals is dramatically lower than would be expected based on the burden of disease.[11] This contributes to an overall cycle of lower funding, less money for research, fewer overall scientific discoveries, as well as a belief within medicine that not much is happening within psychiatry since they rarely hear about any new research.

Finally, cultural ideas about how mental illness looks and the perceived dangerousness of the mentally ill can cause community leaders to make decisions such as blocking the establishment of a residential treatment facility within the community. Even when these are desperately needed, after the amount of pushback in higher SES communities with the resources to do so, they tend to eventually be built in poorer areas where residents don't have as much power to resist. [12] This does two things: It forces people who need treatment to leave their own communities, and it locates people most vulnerable to environmental triggers like drug use or violence directly into communities where this is the norm *even if they didn't live there to start with.*

Stigma as a Barrier to Insight

For me, and for our purposes here, the background of systemic misunderstandings and discrimination is upsetting and adds to the burden people with mental illnesses and their loved ones are already dealing with. But there's also something more insidious about stigma and more directly relevant to our purposes here—stigma against mental illness can be a huge reason people with mental illnesses don't seek care. We've already touched on this idea, but it's so important that I want to go into detail with one more example.

People with mental illnesses aren't immune or unaware of the ideas society in general have about people with mental illness. Studies have shown even individuals with psychosis (typically the most severe and visible form of mental illness) are aware of cultural beliefs singling them out as if they are somehow "lesser," have a high degree of concern about monitoring their behavior to stay within "normal boundaries," and tend to avoid others and isolate themselves in an attempt to avoid social rejection. [12] If even people with severe psychotic illness who have lost touch with our reality and are currently mostly engrossed in their own world of secret societies or conspiracies are still able to both notice and be influenced by social pressures, how strongly are the rest of us affected?

A lot of people who know they suffer from and are receiving treatment for their mental illnesses, especially those in the public eye or in high-level careers where they feel their job or professional reputation may be at risk, struggle with how much to disclose to those around them about their mental health. It's a very difficult thing to navigate, even in the best of situations with the most supportive of people, let alone the rest of the time. But stigma can also play a more insidious role in preventing insight.

This has been referred to as the "package deal" of labeling,[11] and I've seen it play out in devastating ways over and over again. It boils down to this: *In order to accept help for your mental illness, you need to be willing to see yourself as someone who is mentally ill.*

For people with strong lifelong beliefs about how the mentally ill are lazy, unstable, "just overdramatic," unable to care for others, unable to perform well at their jobs, or just plain dangerous or crazy, asking for help puts them in the position of having to apply those labels and negative attributes to themselves (or at the very least, consider how other people will do so). This can result in significant treatment delays or denial of illness, even in people who are aware effective treatment exists and are often even supportive of it *for other people*—just those that are "actually crazy," not themselves.

Most commonly in my experience with the anxiety disorders, this denial manifests as complete rejection of any mental-health diagnosis, attempts to self-manage even severe symptoms at home (the "rough patch"), or at its worst, refusal of any mental-health evaluation or treatment and insistence on continuing to pursue a physical explanation for their symptoms. All the while, even more and more doctors suggest an anxiety or depression explanation. This can continue basically indefinitely. Some patients will refuse to talk to a psychiatrist and be angry with any doctor who suggests it or offers medication with mood effects (even if it's one of the ones that also helps with pain in the absence of psychiatric illness). Sometimes they continue to jump between doctors and specialty centers while getting more and more invasive testing for years, continuing to suffer with their symptoms the entire time.

It's hard to watch. Especially when you're certain the underlying issue is anxiety or depression, regardless of how many tests are run, no other explanation is going to be found, and you're holding the prescription for a medication and/or number for a therapist that would help them significantly, if only they would try it. Even as a professional, it's almost impossible to help someone who has no insight into their condition and either insists nothing is wrong or insists some other mysterious explanation exists, and doctors just can't find it. It also makes them particularly vulnerable to an entire industry of unregulated supplements and snake oil salesmen who insist modern medicine doesn't know anything, but they know a bunch of people who had the same symptoms "disappear" with "Vitamin D."

I'll be the first to admit these can be frustrating situations with patients. I chose this profession to help people. This situation is the worst kind of not being able to help. Even in instances with a terminally-ill patient where nothing I can do will change the fact they're dying, I can still find ways to help. I can talk the family through what happens next and what that person would have wanted. I can take the lines and tubes out of them. I can give them medications to keep them comfortable and ease the fear. I can do *something* to improve the situation somehow. When a patient insists on another explanation for their fatigue and muscle pains other than the obvious one sitting in front of us, there's not much I can do to help. It's the rough equivalent of having horrible heart disease that's limiting your everyday ability to walk up the single flight of stairs into your apartment, doctors wanting to place a stent which would help you significantly, and you refusing and insisting that nothing is wrong with your heart, the problem is something else, look harder. While there may be other things going on as well, I know you're not going to feel much better until I at least fix this very obvious heart problem (in this example). And I want you to feel better.

You often hear hints that stigma may be driving some of this kind of denial reaction while you're having these conversations with patients. I say, "I really believe some of your physical symptoms may be caused by an anxiety disorder," and get an immediate, "I'm not crazy!" in return. I attempt to explain I don't think anyone is crazy. What I do believe is there are very real physical symptoms being caused by an overactive fight or flight system making the hormones in the brain go a bit haywire and cause things like muscle aches (from unconsciously tensing up muscles), fatigue (similarly from constantly being over alert), difficulty concentrating (due to elevations in stress hormones), and a whole host of other things. We often still never really move past the "I'm not crazy," to being able to talk about what I can offer to help.

At the end of the day, most people who fall into this cycle are, in addition to those whose mental illness is diagnosed and treated as such, also victims of the mental-health stigma. They are often willing to try anything in the world to fix their symptoms: heat, cold, pills, injections, sprays, essential oils, you name it—except a medication or a few months of therapy with a decent chance of helping and minimal risk of side effects aimed at a psychiatric condition. Why is that? Often it's their own (sometimes entirely unconscious) stigma against the mentally ill and their inability to mentally place themselves in that group that prevents them from getting desperately-needed help.

One of the most powerful ways I can help those patients (and everyone else) is to change the common perception of what people struggling with mental illness look like, act like, and are able to do with their lives. I've been open about my own struggles with my classmates and colleagues (doctors aren't immune to holding biases and are actually statistically less likely than patients to seek help for their own mental-health problems) throughout my medical training in the hope of helping to provide an alternate picture of what mental illness can look like. I've been approached with questions several times from colleagues struggling on their own and worried about the professional implications of getting mental-health treatment. For doctors or other medical professionals reading this, there really aren't any. Please get help if you need it. It hasn't been an issue for me (or any of my professional patients) yet. Although I'm not oblivious to the idea that someone could hold it against me because of her own prejudices about mental illness, I firmly believe my experiences make me a better doctor, not a worse one.

Changing the picture is an important goal of this book. I hope the varied perspectives and experiences laid out here encourage you to think about your own beliefs and consider the picture in your mind about the face of mental illness.

Part II

JOURNEYS TO INSIGHT:
STORIES FROM EVERYDAY PEOPLE

Nicole: Complicated Relationships

My anxiety and I have always had a complicated relationship. As I've gotten it under better control in the past few years, rather than simplifying it, it became more complex. Anxiety isn't the only mental-health condition I've struggled with. I've had major depressive episodes since I was a teenager. For me, my depression is easier to understand and compartmentalize. When the depression comes for me, it arrives quickly and with little warning. I've gone through this enough that I can recognize the signs early and notice when all of a sudden, things just seem wrong. I talk to my doctor, make medication changes and wait for it to pass. It's not a fun time, but it's transient and after taking things a little slower for a month or two, I'm usually back to "normal." My relationship with depression is painful and littered with relapses, but it's not complicated. For the most part, when we're together I'm miserable, but the rest of the time, we're virtual strangers.

Anxiety, on the other hand, affects my life every day and has for as far back as I can remember. For a long time, the severity of my anxiety went unrecognized and untreated causing it to manifest in different ways. Now that I'm more tuned in to what my anxiety looks and feels like when it's getting worse, I have some insight into when I'm controlling my anxiety and when my anxiety is controlling me, but the lines can still be blurry.

More so than a lot of other mental illnesses, anxiety is not only a disorder—it's a personality trait. My anxiety has been responsible for some of the worst moments of my life. It is also the reason I am a doctor.

To some degree, anxiety and anxious behaviors are normal in little kids. The entire world is new and scary. There are new people, new rules, and new situations every day. Fearing it all is developmentally normal. We mark the age that babies develop "stranger danger" and stop letting strangers hold them as a developmental milestone. Compounding this normal kid stuff, my father was in a serious car accident, hospitalized for a while, and permanently partially disabled when I was five. A little more fear of certain things in the immediate aftermath was probably normal. But in the years between five and eight (when anxious behaviors often start to manifest in kids who will ultimately struggle with anxiety), it morphed into something else entirely.

I was afraid of everything. *All the time.* Not a little scared of everyday situations, but like barricade doors at night to ward off the murderers, freak out if someone was five minutes late coming home because I thought they were dead, spending hours unable to sleep at night listening to every little noise in the house, terrified of everything. Columbine was around the time I started elementary school. Then 9/11 was two years later and given our location in New York, this was an added major source of fear and stress for me (and everyone around me).

As an adult, I understand 9/11 was hardly the first act of terrorism on U.S. soil. There was never any realistic hope of it being the last. I'm also able to wrap my mind around why these things happen in general and the odds of them happening to me or someone that I love, specifically, are statistically close to zero. As an already anxious kid, the world appeared to be burning to the ground. Literally…given the footage of NYC in flames played hour after hour on TV and on the cover of every newspaper for months. There really wasn't any reason offered other than some form of generic "bad people" explanation. I can't say there was a better way to explain acts of terror and complex international politics to a child in elementary school. I can't think of one. But I vividly recall not understanding why the world was just carrying on without everyone looking over their shoulders all the time. The presence of evil or even just unstable people in the world wasn't news to anyone over the age of 10, but it was to me. What had happened to my dad was an accident. It still scared me a lot, but it seemed like something that was theoretically preventable if you were careful enough. The fact that there were people out there with guns or bombs actively trying to hurt us for no real reason wasn't something I was able to cope with or understand.

I never wanted to be away from my parents. I liked staying home where I felt safest. If forced to leave the house, I put stuffed animals and things I cared about into the fireproof safe. I was absolutely sure the house was going to blow up every time I left it. I can't for the life of me explain what exactly was going through my head in these moments, but I vividly remember the fear. I needed things to go according to a schedule. I panicked if anyone was running late or diverted from the stated plan, as it was clearly a sign of impending disaster. I was hyper vigilant of my surroundings to an extent that in retrospect, as a professional, was likely consistent with elements of PTSD.

In addition to my fears of random people trying to kill me, after I learned what anaphylaxis was, I started experiencing a new sensation. It was feeling like my throat was closing at random times, which progressed to a panic attack feeling that I wasn't able to breathe a few times a week. It was alarming for all involved but basically got thrown into the pile of mysterious things going on with me at the time. The pediatrician gave me an inhaler, which if you've never used one, is basically a dose of inhaled adrenaline and literally the last thing someone working themselves up into a panic attack, with no history of asthma, needs.

As my mom talks about in-depth, it wasn't like my parents were doing nothing about any of this. I saw plenty of doctors. Even the ones who were sympathetic and listened to her concerns often defaulted to some form of "Hmm. Yeah. The anxiety sounds a little concerning. But physically she seems okay. Maybe think about therapy? But I mean, she doesn't have behavior problems, gets great grades, and has some friends, so how big of an issue could it be?" I saw therapists intermittently. They never seemed to really help me. Eventually, around the start of middle school—I just stopped mentioning the fears and anxiety to anyone. From all outside appearances, it had gotten better with age as some doctors had suggested it might.

In my own internal world, the anxiety wasn't better, I was just embarrassed and stayed quiet about it. Over the next few years, although I stopped expressing anxious thoughts out loud, I developed physical symptoms common in kids with severe anxiety problems. I was exhausted all the time. I had a lot of stomach issues. I had low blood pressure and passed out from time to time, a ton of muscle pain and terrible headaches, and a lot of very nonspecific things I now recognize to be very common medical presentations of kids with raging anxiety or mental-health problems bubbling below the surface.

Again, we saw all the doctors, including a bunch of specialists in New York City. I was handed diagnoses like candy. None of them came with treatments or even actionable ideas for symptom control. I don't remember being asked very often, if ever, about anxiety or depression during these evaluations. More and more tests were run. More medical jargon was used. And I became more and more convinced something was medically very wrong with me that doctors were unable to find. I was convinced I was in danger of dying. I missed an insane amount of school. None of the pediatric specialists we saw had any answers other than "nothing seems wrong with the organ that I specialize in—maybe try another kind of doctor?"

As I paid more and more attention to and focused more on

these physical symptoms, I noticed more things "wrong" and had more symptoms to report. It was a fairly unproductive spiral of referrals to one new kind of specialist after another who could "maybe weigh in as well."

I started seeing a therapist at some point during all of this for what seemed to be a separate issue after I told my mom that I thought I was suicidal. As a disclaimer, I tell this story to demonstrate the depths and absurdity of my anxiety at the time with no intention to minimize the struggles of those with suicidal thoughts or impulses. I've never personally been suicidal, but helping patients who struggle with this is a part of my professional life and not something I take lightly.

At the time, I made this statement about suicide to Mom, who was, of course, incredibly freaked out and rushed me to a therapist. I had never shown any symptoms of depression and denied being depressed in any way. I was adamant that I didn't want to end my life. I was, in fact, terrified of dying. Since I had learned about the existence of suicide, it became a concern. I was afraid I would somehow unintentionally end my own life. Not because I wanted to die but because I was legitimately terrified of anything that I could die from and now suicide was on that list. I struggled to see how little sense this made. After what appeared to be a very confusing hour for the therapist, we had a chat about how I could just, you know, not hurt myself since it wasn't like I wanted to anyway. She was able to explain to me ways I could get help immediately if I ever felt like this was becoming a more common or concerning thought for me. I was reassured and that was the end of it. She never mentioned seeking medical help for my anxiety.

We returned to our new normal. I had a series of nearly endless physical complaints and pain. I missed a decent amount of school. Doctors didn't offer help so we started to seek out fewer specialists. I still couldn't really sleep. My emotions were more all over the place than you'd expect (even for a teenager). But I kept getting good grades and doing the normal middle school things, so we just carried on with our lives.

By all outward appearances, my anxiety vanished into thin air by the time I reached high school. I still had countless random physical symptoms, but I dealt with them. Completely by accident, I found a method of coping with my anxiety that allowed me to be functional. I never stopped moving. I went to high school full time, took all the honors and AP classes (stacking extras into things like lunch periods), joined or ran a bunch of clubs, and worked 20 to 40 hours a week (generally something like Tues/Wed/Fri/Sun nights and all day on Saturday) in a restaurant throughout it all. When summer hit, I worked as a camp counselor during the day and at the restaurant at night. When I turned 16 and got my license, it became easier to keep myself in nonstop motion. Although it sounds like a miserable time, I had never been happier. Keeping myself that busy, especially the pace of both my school day and restaurant work kept my mind so busy I didn't have a ton of time or energy to devote to anxiety. It got pushed to the side with everything else I was doing.

This served me well. By high school graduation, I was salutatorian, headed to a great college with a good scholarship, had a solid group of friends, and (as a result of my improved control over my own emotions) had better relationships with my family than I had since I was a young child. But as is a common story of untreated or undertreated mental illness, what goes up eventually comes down.

The constant motion thing became impossible to maintain in college. I wasn't working. My classes took up time, but not really that much in the scheme of life and, if we're being honest, most of my freshman year, classes were not all that difficult. I was having panic attacks. I was living with a roommate (who I did not get along with very well) in a tiny box. I had nowhere to hide and nowhere I could reliably be alone. I was trying to make new friends and be "cooler" and less nerdy than I was in high school, which was also hard and kind of stressful.

I was drinking…a lot. And not even because I wanted to. I always had a low tolerance for alcohol and am pretty quick to start throwing up and feeling like crap after a few drinks. But especially at my school, it seemed like the thing to do if you wanted to stay busy and kill some time. I was also incredibly anxious about making new friends, a relatively quiet introvert by nature, and I thought the alcohol made me more likeable. It definitely made hanging out with new people less stressful. In retrospect, I'd probably had two major depressive episodes before college, but I had always just attributed them to various "things going on right now," and I had still never been diagnosed or treated for depression (or anxiety). But my overall current situation at the time, the inability to have any alone time and significant involvement of alcohol, made the episode that hit the fall of my freshman year the most intense in my life.

I have limited memories of that time. Five years later and in a stable headspace, I'm tearing up as I write this. Suffice to say, it was bad. *Really bad.* I think I've blocked much of it out. I wasn't leaving my room unless forced. I went to the classes I couldn't get away with skipping. My relationship with my roommate further deteriorated as I lay on my bed watching "Grey's Anatomy" on my laptop for the half of the day that I wasn't sleeping. I had a group of friends I made early in the year, but I pulled away from them and convinced myself they had never liked me anyway (they had just been being nice). Engrossed in their own freshman year chaos, they didn't chase me or check on me for very long after I drifted away.

I would like to say this was the point at which it was so obvious to me that I wasn't functioning that I got myself into some form of mental healthcare, but it wasn't. In the depths of it, my thinking wasn't clear enough to realize I needed help. I wasn't thinking about the future. I was simply existing. I did most of my schoolwork. I got okay grades. The semester ended, and I went home for the holidays. By the time I returned to school, it had been about four months since my depression started (which I now know to be about the length of a typical untreated depressive episode), and it just kind of faded away.

Almost two years later, the depression was still gone, but my anxiety had progressed to the point where I was having full-blown

"I'm pretty sure I'm dying right now" panic attacks and ending up in the emergency room. It was at this point I was finally referred to a psychiatrist. He was pretty quickly able to figure out what was going on and explain it to me in a way that helped me understand what had been going on over the past few years. His theory was straightforward and made sense to me: I had been dealing with severe anxiety for most of my life but prior to college, I had found ways to cope that kept me functional. The dramatic disruption to my life and old routines when I started college challenged my ability to handle the anxiety, and it got out of control. He explained it was common for people with anxiety disorders, especially undertreated anxiety disorders, to later have major depressive episodes, and together we were able to identify several periods in my life where it seemed like I had experienced those as well.

He started me on medication and referred me to a therapist. But most importantly to me at the time, he did an incredible job contextualizing all of this and reassuring me this was all fixable stuff. I was about to start applying to medical school, which wasn't exactly a stress-free endeavor. I asked him if he thought that would still be possible and to this day, I remember him smiling and almost starting to laugh, before saying, "At least borderline pathological anxiety is practically a requirement for becoming a doctor. You'll be fine. You've spent years considering the worst-case scenarios all the time and trying to do what you can to avoid them? That's medicine in a nutshell."

I've had my ups and downs since then, but overall, my anxiety and depression have remained reasonably well controlled, even through the stresses of medical school and medical residency. Looking back, I still have a hard time understanding how I was able to live with that level of raging anxiety for so long without realizing something was wrong. I remember the things I was thinking and doing, but the intense fear and emotion driving those things is so foreign to me now that the actions no longer make sense. *Even the little things.* I remember getting out of bed to check that the doors (including my bedroom door) were locked several times a night for years. I know why I was doing it, I remember it was fear driving it, and I wasn't able to sleep otherwise. At the time, it seemed reasonable. If I just went and checked, I'd be able to sleep. *No harm done.* To me now, that whole routine sounds tiring, pointless, and more than a little bit paranoid. I also now know that if I start getting the urge to check things like that, it may be a sign my anxiety is starting to get worse, and I need to talk with my doctor.

That ability to notice what's happening and course-correct has been one of the biggest differences for me since that first appointment with the psychiatrist in New Orleans. I now understand what's happening when my anxiety or depression are acting up, what the signs are, and what it starts to look like, and most importantly, I'm able to do something about it.

I have a love-hate relationship with my anxiety. It caused me insurmountable grief and pain for a lot of years before I was able to tamper it down to a manageable level. But I believe the level of anxiety I had about things being medically wrong with me drove my early and persistent interest in science, the human body, and ultimately medicine. I'm almost certain anxiety is, in no small part, why I'm a doctor. I'm also sure the experiences I've had struggling with anxiety and my ability to understand, on some level, what my patients are experiencing makes me a better doctor. While I wouldn't wish my anxiety disorder on anyone, without it, I'm not sure that I would have found my way to a career I love or that I would have the privilege of spending my days helping people struggling with all forms of mental illness.

As I said, our relationship is complicated.

Lori: Mission Impossible

"My mother gave me life and never asked
for anything in return. That is her secret you know,
always giving without any expectations. She is as constant
as the sunrise, the moon, the stars, and I count on her.
She helps me find my way through the years and
makes me laugh while doing it. There are
some things only a mother can do."
—*Unknown*

My childhood nickname was "Lightning." I am told it was because you never knew where I would strike next. As an adult, I intend to use my powers for good and strike down the stigma surrounding mental health.

As I sat down to write for this book, I found myself thinking about my life while staring at a blank computer screen. *Where do I start? What do I want to say? What happened to me that is noteworthy? What can I share that will help or inspire others?* It felt so personal, like exposing your soul for the world to see and judge.

I found it emotionally challenging to sift through the private details of my life and decide what to be open about and share. It was daunting.

So, naturally I procrastinated and turned on the radio for background noise and willed myself to write something. Anything. As I began, the Miranda Lambert song, "This Ain't Your Mama's Broken Heart" started playing. I confess, I love country music and cowboys. I grew up on a horse farm in upstate New York, competed in horse shows, joined 4-H clubs and went to rodeos and square dances.

The lyrics, "Hide your crazy and start acting like a lady. You have to keep it together even when you are falling apart," caught my attention. I stopped and thought, *why can't others know you're falling apart? Because your family, friends, or society can't handle it? Because it makes them uncomfortable? Who decided "they" are more important than you? Than me? Who are they anyway? Why the hell do we care?*

This song reminded me of my prior generation's belief that mental illness was something you didn't talk about. It was shameful. It was a weakness. Back then, all that mattered was the appearance of normal (whatever that is). I thought of my mother. This had certainly been true for her in her lifetime.

My story starts with my mom, Carolann. As a mother myself, I now appreciate the courage, energy, and resilience it takes to live each day worrying about your child's safety and happiness. For me, it's paramount. My kids are my greatest joy and my biggest cause for concern. Worrying whether they are healthy, happy, safe, and successful is my first thought in the morning and my last thought at night. It is with me every day, all day, ever present.

I am not an overly-religious person, but I pray for my children to have long, healthy lives filled with safety, security, love, friendship, peace, success, adventure, and fun every night before I go to sleep. I also pray for them whenever I am worried about them or they are struggling. It makes me feel like I have called in back-up to help protect them.

My mother believed deeply in prayer. She read her *Bible* every day until dementia took over. She has vascular dementia due to a heart condition and a series of strokes. Her short-term memory has faded, but she still loves listening to music and coloring. Strangely, she remembers the words to songs and hymns.

I am her daughter. This is one of the last things she knows, most days. I can't help her remember. She can no longer provide me emotional support or advice. But we can eat a donut, color, and share a laugh together. Each day, when I say goodbye, she grabs my hand and says, "Go safe."

The impact undiagnosed and untreated lifelong mental-health issues had on my mother and her physical and mental health is undeniable. She spent a great deal of my childhood in the hospital. I always suspected her physical issues had an underlying component of mental-health issues. My father recently admitted that my mom spent time in a mental-health institution.

Mom struggled after my older sister was born. She was depressed and couldn't get out of bed. Today, this would be diagnosed and treated as postpartum depression. In the 1960s, it was so misunderstood, that she was committed to the Mid-Hudson Psychiatric Center! I am aware of what happened in those institutions. It breaks my heart thinking about how she suffered, especially while being depressed and separated from her new baby. How in the world did professionals in my lifetime consider this treatment? I consider it cruel.

Sometimes now when I am visiting Mom at the nursing home, she suddenly looks panicked and asks "What did I do wrong? Was I bad again? Is that why I am here?" In those moments, I believe she is remembering being in the psychiatric center. All I can do is reassure her that she is safe and didn't do anything wrong. I tell her she is in a rehabilitation center, and she is doing great. I tell her I love her. She relaxes, smiles, and goes back to her coloring while I try not to cry. I hope during this current quarantine of 2020 while I am locked out and can't see her that the staff is reminding her she is safe and that I exist. It has already been nine weeks since I have been allowed to see her. It breaks my heart. I hope I get to see her again.

I don't recall ever feeling judged by my mother. She accepted me for me, imperfections and all. I remember in middle school I got caught cutting class. I needed a note signed by a parent. I didn't want to tell my father who was a junior high school science teacher and took these things seriously. Mom was in the hospital recovering from a broken neck as the result of a car accident (I now wonder about that accident and if it was in fact an accident). I rode my bike to the hospital, and she signed the note. When I left, she told me to take my education more seriously because it mattered. She knew this because she never really had the chance to get one. She didn't mention it again. But I assure you, she couldn't have been more proud when I graduated high school with honors and a regent's diploma.

There didn't seem to be anything I could do to make her stop loving me...even later in life when my husband made it clear she wasn't welcome in our house unless specifically invited which prevented her from visiting and seeing her grandchildren. She did her best to understand and not make my situation worse. She knew I was trying to keep the peace at home and in my marriage. I would bring the kids to her house whenever my husband was out for the day so she could spend time with them. She loved crocheting, painting, drawing, coloring, and any kind of art and spent hours with them playing and doing crafts. She truly enjoyed their time together. She made clothes for my daughter's Barbie dolls and my son's stuffed animals. I still have them today. Often, when Nicole was seized by a panic attack or struggling, and I was exhausted from trying to calm her down, I would tell her to go to her room and call her grandmother. They would talk for hours. Nicole was distracted and calmed down, Mom was happy, and I had some time to focus on my son and husband.

When I was fifteen, my mother moved to Long Island. As an adult, I understand how almost impossible that must have been for her. I now appreciate what it takes to get to the point where you leave your marriage. To risk that kind of change, even when your marriage is toxic or abusive, is hard. Even after she moved out, she was on a mission to ensure she stayed in my life.

Back in the 1980s, at least once a month, as I left high school and then community college, there she was sitting in the parking lot waiting to take me to lunch. Although I was hurt and felt abandoned, she couldn't be deterred by my teenage anger. Mom continued to drive up from Long Island to see me. She came home for the holidays and never gave up. I eventually went to college at Hofstra on Long Island, a few miles from where she lived. Then we spent a great deal of time together. She has always been there for me in any way she was capable. Often, it was in the background, and early in life, I started taking care of her more than the other way around, but I came to understand it was everything she had to give. I never doubted she loved me.

Our connection was enough. It formed a foundation for what I value the most as a parent. Give everything you got and try not to judge. Unconditional love and acceptance.

Mom was born in 1938 and endured a difficult childhood. Her parents were the only divorced family in the small town where she grew up. It was considered odd and shameful and made her different, weird. She shared painful stories about her childhood. She was bullied and struggled in school and was told she was stupid. She believed this. She did not know until she was an adult that she had dyslexia.

When she was very young, her mother's doctor told her mom she needed to go away and "restore" herself. My grandmother's doctor was close to hospitalizing (committing) her as he believed she was on the verge of a breakdown. (Today, this isn't even a diagnosis). I believe there were also domestic abuse issues. She left alone and came back several years later but couldn't care for her daughter. My mom was raised by a relative who did her best but struggled with serious alcoholism, and then she moved around and lived with various relatives. The good news is she later reconciled with her mother.

Mom experienced abandonment, trauma, bullying, abuse, and

neglect, resulting in lifelong general and social anxiety issues. These went undiagnosed, unspoken, and untreated as was expected back then. Her anxiety manifested in physical symptoms and illnesses—both real and perceived—that defined most of her life.

I share my mother's genetics. Surprise! I have anxiety. Mine presents around a constant fear about my kids' safety and a compulsion to solve every problem they encounter. I obsess over the most minuscule issue my kids have or could have. I cannot tolerate them being the slightest bit sad, upset, or ill.

I take the saying, "You can only be as happy as your unhappiest child," to a whole new level. As my kids grew, I tried to protect them from distress. I intervened to shield them from criticism, rejection, and hardship both within and outside our home. I would lay awake at night fixated on the most unlikely dangers lurking in their future.

I attribute my worrying to being a mom, but we all know there is more to it. My entire life, I have, on occasion, had trouble taking a deep breath. As a teenager, my doctor told me it was probably because of my scoliosis. He said my spine presses on my lungs. Interesting theory? I now recognize it happens when I am anxious or stressed.

I still worry a lot. I struggle to say no and prioritize myself. I saw a therapist after my divorce. We explored why I stayed so long in my marriage. It wasn't for financial reasons since I was the one working. She encouraged me to consider self-care and put myself first, at least sometimes and helped me explore past trauma and its possible impact on my hesitancy to feel justified standing up for what I need or want and to understand my compulsion to try to fix everything and control it so everyone will be happy. I spend most of my time worrying about everyone else's happiness and needs. A possible working theory is, I believe they are more deserving and have more value than I do.

As a child, I was molested by my piano teacher. This childhood trauma may have contributed to some of these issues. I am working on giving myself permission to say and pursue what I want, believe, or need. It is not okay to let people be physically or emotionally abusive, critical, or take advantage of you. I deserve to be appreciated, respected, and accepted for who I am. By the way, so do you! My therapist was the first professional in my life (besides my daughter) to tell me I suffer from anxiety and depression. I think of myself as an independent, strong, action-oriented, and optimistic person. I raised wonderful children, financially supported my family, took care of my parents, and built a strong network of amazing friends. I am truly blessed. My mission to eliminate anxiety from my children's lives wasn't a success, but it was never a practical or even necessary mission. I now realize it is a part of who they are, and I wouldn't change them for the world. My goal now is to support them and trust they have the knowledge, treatment, and skills to be happy. I pray they know they are my life.

Wendy: On Your Mark, Get Set, Go

I've heard people say "things run in the family," like the bad knees and nearsightedness I inherited from my mom. Anxiety walks, not runs, through my family. It's not in a rush. It doesn't begin with the bang of a starting gun and a "on your mark, get set, go!" It doesn't give you a pre-warning it's coming for you, and it doesn't notify you when it's arrived.

I can't pinpoint the exact moment it entered my life, the moment it began to influence me, or even the cumulative effect it's had on my choices over the years. But like an old friend, anxiety has always been there. Not only for me, but also, for almost everyone around me.

I've seen its effects first-hand in my paternal grandmother, my father, his sister, my sister, her children, my daughter, and my grandchildren. It's not exactly what I would *choose* to pass on in my gene pool. Although it affects almost all of us, it does so in different ways. Its effects are subtly entangled in our genetics, our personalities, our experiences, and our interactions with each other. The generations before mine didn't talk about these kinds of things—anxiety and mental illness. They hid them. Or they called them "eccentricities" and shrugged them off. Those in my generation do talk about it, and we share the ways we've found to help deal with it. There isn't one thing that can help all of us. We all experience our anxiety differently. But having people that, on some level, understand us and don't judge us makes all the difference in being able to cope with this affliction.

My sister is agoraphobic. Thankfully, it is not so extreme she can't leave her home at all. She's pretty comfortable in her own small town or out in the company of others whom she trusts. Although she knows how to drive and has a driver's license, she avoids it because it triggers anxiety attacks. This puts her at the mercy of others to get around and places limits on her independence…on a good day. On a bad day, it can take situations that someone without anxiety would find stressful and escalate them to a crisis-level situation.

Once, she was sure her husband was having a heart attack. She lived less than two miles from the hospital. No one else was home. She felt she had no choice but to drive him to the emergency room herself, which of course, caused her an incredible amount of panic and quickly clouded her judgment, preventing her from being able to think or plan clearly.

Less than two blocks from home she spotted an acquaintance walking down Main Street. She actually stopped the car and tried to convince the poor man, who knew nothing of her fears of driving and had a suspended license himself, to take over driving for her and get them to the hospital.

Her husband, lying across the back seat and still having severe chest pains, managed to coax her to keep driving. Very cautiously. What should have been a two-minute drive down 55 mph back roads to the hospital became a twenty-minute odyssey of absolute terror and panic for them both. To top it off, her husband was indeed having a heart attack.

They got to the hospital in time. The hospital staff was able to help her husband and diffuse a situation that had began as "My husband is having some chest pain, and we're worried it may be a heart attack," at home but morphed into a screaming woman on the knife's edge of a panic attack by the time they finally arrived at the hospital.

Everything worked out that time. Her husband is fine. She hasn't yet been in another situation in which she felt like her safety or her loved one's safety was dependent upon her ability to drive. But the whole experience hasn't done much to decrease her fear of driving or of being in unfamiliar settings. Many of us also share and validate these fears.

I am deathly afraid to drive in snow storms or high winds, and white-knuckle it the whole way if I find myself having to drive home in a storm. My grandson doesn't even want to learn to drive, my daughter can't handle driving in the rain or snow, and my granddaughter is a very, very careful driver. That, in all honesty, seems like self-preservation to me. To all of us.

One thing I've found within my family is we are all high-strung. We can very easily tell you what the worst-case outcome would be in any given situation. We're also pretty sure that the worst is what is about to happen.

From the moment I hear the words "chest pain" out of your mouth, you are 100% already dead to me. You are having a heart attack, and it will kill you. Probably today. If not, maybe after a long and painful hospital stay. Either way, I am going to keep worrying and keep imagining progressively more horrifying ways that this will play out until either: you actually die, *or* I've convinced myself that since all six medical personnel I've questioned so far seem to agree that you're fine, and you're sitting up in bed telling me you're fine, and the hospital wants to send you home, that it seems unlikely that you will suddenly drop dead now. You'll probably live until your next heart attack, at least. I'm sure there will be another.

Since I spent all this time between the "chest pain" and the point when I'm convinced you're not actually dying right this second preparing for the worst, I am acutely aware of all of the possible things that could go wrong at any given time. I've been watching, waiting, considering, catastrophizing. I've made decisions. I'd call your sister to tell her first. I'd rather she calls your mom than me. I think she'd rather hear it from her. I'd stay in the house right now, but come next winter, I might prefer something smaller without snow to shovel. I should probably move somewhere with more reliable public transportation anyway without you around to drive me.

This kind of endlessly and obsessively planning for the worst may be a valuable survival skill the one percent of the time the worst actually does happen. The problem is the other 99% of the time. The 99 times when it's not your heart, when we're released from the hospital four hours later with some antacid. It would have been a stressful day for anyone, I guess, but I'm falling-over exhausted. And none of it is from anything that actually happened. We sat in a hospital waiting room and watched TV for three hours. There's nothing inherently exhausting about that. But planning exactly how I would handle every aspect of my husband's untimely death? Mentally living those next weeks over and over again until I felt like I had the best possible plan to handle it? That's a big task for an afternoon.

I've thought about it a lot and believe my particular breed of anxiety is from both my gene pool and childhood trauma and abuse—a nature/nurture double whammy.

When I was three, we moved closer to family. Molestation and sexual abuse at the hands of my "bad grandfather" began and continued for years. I believe this long-term trauma was the start of my life-long struggle to be safe, feel safe, and have self-worth instead of self-blame. Fear for my safety (and the safety of loved ones) has fueled anxiety that has kept me from making choices and taking chances to achieve my goals and dreams. I have always felt I was not good enough and struggled with low self-esteem. I am terrified when anything good happens, as it often seems like something equally bad or worse will happen next, which negates the positive.

As I got a bit older, I lived in a diverse neighborhood, and the kids played outside together, weather permitting. It was like that then. Your mother kicked you out to play, ride your bike, and get fresh air all day. We got along pretty well on the block no matter the ethnicity. Starting school was a whole different thing, however. Most of the kids from the block went to Catholic school, but I went to public school. I was one of a small minority of white kids there and was largely unaccepted and picked on.

I excelled at schoolwork but was pretty socially inept. School tensions continued to drive my anxiety and feelings of being unsafe. I learned to put on a stone face and not show my feelings. I escaped into books; the library was a haven for me. I loved to read and finished up the children's section at a young age. One librarian let me take out books from the adult section after permission from my mother. I also began a pattern of eating for comfort. Fatty, tasty foods seemed to dull painful thoughts and jittery nerves.

Junior high school and high school were rough; there were riots and violence, and you had to be on your guard all the time. Being constantly alert made sense, and self-protection was necessary. Anxiety seemed to be an asset. I learned to size up situations quickly and to use humor to diffuse tension. This carefully-honed skill set of always being on guard and always preparing for the worst hasn't served me as well since then.

Once I graduated from high school, I secured a state job and began taking bookkeeping classes at night. This was a great opportunity for my career. Unfortunately, I had to take the subway to class at night, fears over my safety made it impossible to continue, and despite my disappointment in myself, I quit the class.

I was offered a job with a radio station that sounded like a fun and interesting job with growth potential but I was afraid I wasn't good enough and I would fail. I was frozen with fear and did not even try it. I wanted to be an inventor, but I haven't yet been able to convince myself that I could possibly have any idea that is good enough to succeed. I am afraid I will fail before I try. I am extremely critical of myself and self-sabotage all the time.

I love to read and write. When I was asked to share my viewpoint for this book, I was excited, and I really wanted to contribute. I thought about wanting to do it, but did nothing, again paralyzed by anxious thoughts: *I can't do it well, my ideas are not good enough, my story doesn't matter, it won't help or make sense to others.*

This is what happens in my mind all day, every day. It continues to be a struggle for me. In the real world, I have a good job in human resources working for a human services agency with the goal of helping people lead rewarding lives. Working here gives me the opportunity to support those employees; some of them are therapists and other mental health professionals who understand and help people with mental illnesses. I feel like I am making a positive difference in our employees' lives, helping and supporting them, so they can help our clients.

Being around co-workers who understand anxiety issues are common and treatable gave me the realization and courage to go and get professional help for myself. I went to see a psychiatrist and was diagnosed with major depressive and anxiety disorder and prescribed medication. Since I have been reflecting and refocusing on my life story, I realize the positive impact therapy has had on my life, and I also clearly see I still have work to do. Unhealthy habits, like eating comfort foods to dull my senses, are still challenging, but I'm making progress.

I also find that engaging in activities that take me away from my thoughts of being unsafe and unworthy are good ways to find relief, such as reading and solving Sudoku puzzles. Sometimes, doing physical things where my brain goes on autopilot seems to help, like doing the dishes (which has double benefits) while listening to music.

I will never know how much I missed in life due to circumstances and how much was due to my anxiety. They're so entangled. I don't think it's even possible to really know what my life would look like without anxiety.

I have struggled with depression and anxiety for as far back as I can remember. I am proud that I am a survivor, and I'll keep working at making each day one where I feel a little less anxious and a little better about myself. Anxiety, for me, is just a fact of life. If the subject comes up in conversation now, I just smile and say, "I was born that way."

Kristin: Wall of Doom

My anxiety has been a powerful force in my life for as long as I can remember. It's not easy to describe. When anxiety hits, it feels like a giant cement wall mentally blocks me. It causes me to do things like freeze or procrastinate which I know are incredibly counterproductive. My go-to place is seeing the worst-case scenario and if I'm not careful, the anxiety will paralyze me.

I recall one of these moments in college where I was drowning in worry. My friend and I snuck a cat into our dorm room to keep as our pet. No pets were allowed on campus, so we were breaking the rules. One night, out of the blue, I started thinking about how awful it would be if we were caught. Then, the wave of dread rushed over me. What if we do actually get caught? What if we get kicked out of the dorms? How would I continue my education? Would I commute? What would happen to my roommate? Would she have to move back to Connecticut? Would I fail to get my college education? Would I fail at life?

I was awake with these thoughts all night. I knew, on some level, that my worry was way out of proportion. We'd had the cat for two months. I wasn't sure why I was panicking tonight. Yet, the feeling lasted for hours, and I wasn't able to do anything aside from lay in bed with a sick feeling in my stomach, convinced this was the end of my college career. After hours and hours of this, I fell asleep. By morning, although I was able to remember I had been freaking out about the cat the night before, the guttural fear had mostly resolved, and I was able to think more rationally. Even if we got caught, we would figure it out. This was not the worst offense anyone who graduated from my school had ever committed. It probably wasn't even the worst thing someone had done this week.

The problem is, at the onset of these "worry" thoughts, it feels impossible to stop them. I get emotional and cannot control them. Once I think to myself, *so what if something bad happens?* My brain responds by immediately convincing me I will not be able to handle it. It is overwhelming. I can't move past it. The giant cement wall is there, and I can no longer see my way around it. A lot of times, like with the cat, I take the direct route to "panic mode." I think about the future and conjure up all kinds of possible disasters. Then I freak out. I try to calm myself down and tell myself there's no need to worry, but it is too late, as I've already accepted it is a crisis. I have pushed the panic button, and the wall is there standing tall. *Looming.* It is impenetrable.

The panic and the wall are bad enough. But my anxiety then has the ability to create situations to further escalate the panic. I feel like I have a million things to do and no time to do it. All of a sudden, I'll think of something I was supposed to do. I freeze. I wait for that sinking feeling to set in. A wave of panic starts in my stomach and spreads to my entire body. I feel my heart sink. I begin to think of all the worst-case scenarios, and they grow and grow until there is no doubt the only outcome is complete and utter failure.

Once I start thinking about a task I need to complete and the fear sets in, I can no longer focus on anything else. For example, as I'm sitting in science class, I start thinking about my English paper, which is due later in the week. Now I can't focus on anything but that paper. My mind goes into panic mode. I start to obsess about how long the paper needs to be and when I'm going to be able to get it done. I know it isn't possible. I can't get it done. So what is the point? Then comes the procrastination. I put it off because why start if my only option is failure? Why even bother? I would rather sleep and escape the pressure.

Later, after I calm down and am thinking more rationally, I get mad at myself for procrastinating. I realize I would be in a better situation now if I had started the paper earlier, but I just wasn't able to get over the wall. It makes the whole situation worse, since now that the deadline is rapidly approaching, there is actually a reason to panic and a chance I'll go into the whole spiral again.

I haven't yet managed to completely eliminate the waves of panic from my life, but I've found ways to minimize their impact and make that panic button less of an automatic response every time I think of something I need to get done. The anxiety thrives on constant overthinking and overanalyzing. It gives it life, so I try to keep my thoughts in the present. If I start to get overwhelmed, I make lists of the things I need to do, figure out what needs to be done today, and go from there. I only look at one thing at a time. I force myself to believe things can wait until tomorrow. I have a great support system that has helped me to learn to cope with some of the anxiety. My mom is understanding and able to help me talk things through and try to gain perspective before the panic response sets in. She tells me whatever happens, we will handle it together. It's the "we" part that really helps.

Gaining insight that anxiety is part of my life but doesn't have to control my life has been powerful. It has come with time and self-reflection. As I've gotten older and survived tough situations, I have become more able to remind myself I can handle bad, scary things. I have done it before, and I can do it again. Ironically, despite years of my anxiety having been centered around school and deadlines, I've chosen to spend my career in schools. I now feel armed with dynamite, like I have started blasting the cement wall, and I am watching the bricks crumble one by one.

Now that I'm a teacher, I use my own experiences to help students reframe things when they are overwhelmed or "frozen." I understand there are reasons assignments don't get completed on time. It isn't always as simple as laziness. My fear of wanting to do things perfectly prevented me from being able to even start assignments. I now role model coping strategies for my students and teach them that there are ways we can overcome these emotional obstacles together. My life experiences have made me a more compassionate teacher. I teach the coping skills it took me years to master on my own to my students. It is satisfying to offer them a head start on developing their own coping strategies. I tell them we can do this together. I see them growing emotionally, and I know I have made a difference in their lives for years to come.

Tear down that wall!

Breanna: The World is a Stage

I have more scars covering my body than someone should have at my age, probably at any age. Scars cover my arms, chest, back, face, and neck; basically, if you can see my skin, then you can find scars.

Since the sixth grade, I've been compulsively picking my skin. It started when I began getting acne. As soon as I saw a bump, I would try to pop it or scratch it until it was gone, until I could no longer feel a bump at all, until all that was left was a combination of blood and raw, open skin.

I had a vague idea I was damaging my body. The irony of the whole thing was that in trying to rid myself of the original temporary acne bump, I created a more permanent scar. I told myself that I was fine, and the scars would heal.

Even worse, my acne was determined to be entirely related to my sensitive and oily skin. Because I was unable to keep my hands off my face, I was compounding my skin breakouts. What was I doing? Popping and picking and leaving scars and more scars. Why was I doing it? That was unclear. At around the same time in my life, I became the victim of bullying by people I considered friends. These *friends* called me terrible names and made fun of me, but I let them because they were the friends that I had at the time. I think part of the reason why I started picking at my skin so much was due to anxiety fueled from the bullying.

I felt insecure about myself because of the terrible things they said about me and to me. This led to increased insecurities about how I looked, which accelerated my focus and discomfort with all the scars on my face.

Before school, I would have to put on a face full of makeup. I hated putting makeup on. It was such a chore. It was like putting a mask on everyday. I had to get up an hour earlier every day so that I could do my best to smear enough makeup on my face to cover the scars just enough so I could get through the day.

I am thankful my mom and my sister were there to teach me how to properly put on makeup, especially my older sister, who would not let me leave the house looking like a clown. However, you can't really put foundation on your arms and back. So, I would wear a hoodie or sweater so my arms and back would always be covered. This wasn't an ideal permanent solution.

As middle school turned into high school, my picking and the scars from it were tormenting me every day. At school, I already felt uncomfortable and self-conscious, and then my friends would begin their usual name-calling and teasing. It was too much. I would come home from school crying to my mom and my sister because I was so distraught. I was upset all the time. I felt hopeless and depressed.

My family finally said "enough" and brought me to a dermatologist. I wanted to calm my acne down in time for the junior prom. The doctor prescribed topical creams that made my sensitive skin become hypersensitive. I couldn't leave the house without expecting a sunburn even on a cloudy day, or my skin would burn when I would sweat in gym class. Then my skin began to dry out and peel. It hurt. Some nights, I cried because it was so painful, but my acne diminished.

As I had less acne to pick, I tried to figure out why I picked at all. Since I had less acne to blame for the picking, there had to be other reasons. As I paid more attention, I started to realize that I was more prone to "attack" my skin on my arms when they were warm. I started taking an ice cube and running it up and down my arms when I got the urge to pick—when I was hot, when I was stressed, when I was sad, or even when I was bored. This helped. A little bit.

Around my senior year of high school, the fog, in general, seemed to lift. I was picking a little less. I met new people who seemed to really like and accept me. They helped me find the courage to let go of some of the toxic friends I had had for years. These friends became real friends who accept me, support me, and care about me. They are my best friends to this day.

At this point, you are probably wondering what all of this has to do with anxiety. At this point in the story I, myself, wouldn't have drawn a clear connection between my picking and my anxiety except maybe to call it "a nervous habit."

Just recently, I switched dermatologists. Here I was, a sophomore (almost junior) in college still suffering from acne even with the topical medications, still picking my skin all the time. It was one of the hottest days of the year on campus, and I was wearing a jacket over my short-sleeve shirt that I refused to take off. I would rather suffer the heat than show my scarred arm before I got inside the doctor's office.

But with a new doctor, came a new perspective. It didn't take very long for the new doctor to assess the situation. He looked at my skin and immediately said, "You have got to stop picking. Your acne is no longer active, but you are going to have these scars for years to come."

The previous doctor had never asked about anything other than my acne. He'd never mentioned the picking other than to tell me it "wasn't helpful" for my acne. He'd simply treated the acne, not the real problem. This new doctor asked me why I was doing it. He asked me about my acne and my feelings about my acne. He asked me if I knew that the scars were the result of the picking. And he helped me realize the reason I pick is driven by anxiety. This doctor recommended that I go see a cognitive behavior therapist and/or take the anxiety medications.

I have yet to do either of those things. My parents believe that it is just a habit. They think I can stop myself. My mom's method to help when I am home is to say, "No, stop picking!" or give me a look when she sees me going at my skin. She is trying to help. It can help, sometimes, to make me more aware of the picking when I'm just doing it out of habit, when I'm not really paying much attention. But most of the time, I'm aware of what I'm doing. It's just not something that I can control. I can't just stop. Believe me, I would stop if I could. I want to more than anything.

I often feel trapped between these two realities. On one hand, I need to stop picking. On the other hand, I pick when I'm stressed or when I feel guilty. And I feel guilty that I can't stop picking like my family thinks I should be able to, like I think I should be able to. Which only serves to drive me to pick my skin as a form of release. It is a vicious cycle.

When I say that I can't stop, I mean I literally cannot control it. I go into a trance of some kind where I can see my fingers moving but can't stop them until the skin has been picked, and I can feel it. I wasn't sure why I would go into this trance-like state. I would even tell myself it wasn't real. There was no way to explain it to anyone that made sense.

Well, there is an explanation. It just took me ten years to find it. By chance, I stumbled across an article online talking about a body habit disorder known as, *body-focused repetitive behaviors*. I started to cry as I read the article. It was all so familiar. My weird and silent struggle suddenly snapped into focus, became clearer, and became easier to explain.

It is called CSP (compulsive skin picking). It's related to anxiety and can manifest as all kinds of things from skin picking to hair pulling or even nail biting. Reading this personal description of exactly what I am dealing with every day was like lifting a weight off of my shoulders.

To know others suffer like I do made me feel so much better because for years, I thought I was alone. I didn't think anyone could understand or help me. But seeing this, I finally felt understood. Not only did this Internet stranger understand me, she helped me understand myself.

It's still hard. Really hard. Every day. It has been a long and uphill battle feeling like I was fighting against myself. Now here I am, almost ten years later, with answers and a diagnosis and a lot more understanding. That's been revolutionary. But it didn't solve everything overnight.

Will I ever go see a therapist or try anxiety meds? Maybe. I hope I will. If it can help me and bring me some self-confidence, then I'm all for it. I'm still not sure I need therapy or medication to stop picking. I think I'll be able to make myself stop. It helps to have a name for what I'm up against and know other people struggle as well. Now, I'm fighting compulsive skin picking syndrome, which feels easier than fighting my own mind and this weird and shameful thing I do but don't talk about.

I hope sharing my experience and struggle helps others know they aren't alone. I hope it helps others realize there is nothing wrong with them or with who they are as a person. This is just something they are dealing with. I also want everyone to know there is help out there if you want it. I haven't yet decided if I want it, and that's okay, too.

There is no well-defined end to my struggle with anxiety. This is something I live with every day. I don't know when or if it will end. But I can learn more about myself and my options. I can go get treatment if I want it. I am old enough now to make my own decisions about my body and my medical care.

My plan going forward is to love my body and mind with everything I have and to continue openly discussing my struggles so that other people can come to know they're not alone. As of this writing, I am graduating in a few months with a B.A. in stage design, and I am looking forward to a successful, fun career helping to entertain the world. The world's a stage. The possibilities are endless. Design it your way.

Emily: Life Ends on Sunday

I suffered from anxiety my entire life, but until college, I thought this was how everyone felt all the time. I believed it was normal to feel like the world was ending every Sunday as a new school week started. Didn't everyone feel nauseous before they woke up in the morning to go to school or work?

I was the goody-two shoes, the perfect older child; I *had* to get good grades. I was a cheerleader, took voice lessons, performed in the musicals at my high school, ran track, and took art classes and piano lessons. Yet before every game, every performance, every deadline for an art piece, I panicked. I convinced myself I wasn't good enough and was terrified of failing and letting my family and friends down. I thought this was how everyone felt. I thought other people were just better at hiding it.

When I left for college, my anxiety ramped up to a whole new level. Thrown into a different world I knew nothing about, I focused on the one thing I could control: my body. I over-exercised and restricted certain foods, losing a significant amount of weight I didn't need to lose. I obsessed over running a specific number of miles each day and ate the same bland meals repeatedly. I believed I couldn't fail if I micromanaged every aspect of my life. Controlling my food and exercise meant I knew exactly what the result would be. I'd have a perfect body, and everyone would like me and accept me—a flawless plan.

Not surprisingly, my anxiety increased. I avoided outings that involved food and panicked constantly over possibly missing a workout, dreading not getting X number of miles in each week. Family and friends were getting increasingly concerned and, finally, I was forced to take a semester off from college to go home to recover.

I was heartbroken. I had failed. I couldn't even manage to go to college like a "normal" young adult. Now, I was going to miss out on everything.

Although that semester off was when my recovery started, it took me a lot longer to understand what my anxiety really was, how it was affecting my life, and how it was driving my eating disorder.

A significant catalyst for my anxiety is change. Before every job I'd ever started (as well as throughout), I worried my coworkers would see me for what I was: a fraud. I wasn't good enough, and I sure as hell wasn't smart enough. My college degrees and perfect grades meant nothing to me. I told myself *my classes were easy! Anyone could've gotten the good grades I did if they had my major. I got lucky!* I wanted to curl up in bed instead, too afraid to try something new and fail.

The anxiety I felt in middle and high school each morning carried over to college and persisted when I started working full-time. My anxieties of failing hid behind my worries about when I would work out, if I'd have to wake up early to fit it in, and if I'd even *want* to work out that day. I stressed over what I'd eat and if there'd be food at my job. Every morning, I was plagued with fear and anxiety, afraid of what the day would bring. Normally the anxiety subsided once I started the workday, but I still over-thought everything I did and never trusted myself fully. This is something I still struggle with to this day.

Stress and anxiety were causing me to feel nauseous all the time; with my stomach bloating so much, it was uncomfortable. I had racing thoughts. I would get into funks where I was depressed and moody. In the beginning of my recovery, when I was feeling anxious, I would fixate on what I was eating and what my workouts would be. I labeled my "healthy" foods so no one else would eat them. I obsessively planned my workouts a week in advance.

Eventually, when I found myself feeling anxious, my therapist tried to teach me to sit with my feelings to help see what I was really worried about and whether or not I could pinpoint why I was feeling anxious. I learned that I would simply have to "feel the feelings" in order to let my anxiety pass rather than trying to bury them in tight control over my eating.

This was easier said than done. There were many times I broke down crying, afraid of what would happen if I let myself give up control. Food and exercise were my security blankets covering my anxiety of failing at life. The one thing I felt I could control and succeed at, I was told I'd have to give up.

As my recovery progressed, I began to find myself in a cycle of restricting, overeating, and then over-exercising to compensate for how much I had eaten. I started turning to food instead of away from food when I was anxious. Since I prided myself on restricting and over-exercising, overeating was especially shameful for me. Even when I stopped restricting and started incorporating all foods back into my diet, I didn't trust my body enough to eat when it was hungry and stop when it was full.

Before bed, I'd sneak into the pantry and pour myself endless bowls of cereal, using the sweetness as a way to ease my anxiety. I found myself panicking before holiday events where there would be a lot of food, anxious I'd just eat it all. Through lots of therapy and self-care, I was able to move past this period of my recovery. Listening to what my body needed rather than what my anxiety was telling me I wanted, I nourished my body with food and movement that now feels good to me. I learned to tolerate, accept, and love my body for exactly how it is.

Restricting and/or overeating weren't the only ways anxiety was impacting my life, nor were they the most enduring manifestation of my anxiety. I also have a habit of picking at my face when I am feeling overly anxious. I've struggled with skin picking since middle school, which escalated into something much worse as I became a young adult faced with many new changes. Standing in front of the mirror, I'd lean in close and pick…pick…pick.

The feeling of picking at my face brought short-term relief, followed by shame, humiliation, and physical pain. I began to pick so much that I would make myself bleed, giving myself cuts and scars on my face that I tried in vain to cover up with makeup. I would have episodes of intense picking, followed by letting my face heal, only to go back to picking again as soon as my face started to clear up.

I would use pins and needles to pick even deeper.

What exactly was I picking at? I didn't really have acne, but the few pimples I did have were like a gateway drug that led me to picking at my entire face. I would be in so much pain, but I kept doing it anyway. I picked, I bled, I cried, I picked again. I couldn't stop. For years, every time I stepped into the bathroom I leaned towards the mirror, sometimes picking for hours, especially before bed. I picked unconsciously, my fingers gravitating towards my face while watching TV or doing homework.

I was humiliated at how my face looked, ashamed at myself for picking, and longed for a clear face that didn't need makeup. I dreamed about jumping in a pool without worrying about how my face looked or stepping out of the shower with clear skin that wasn't red and blemished. I wanted to wake up next to my husband and not have to run to the bathroom to cover up my scars and redness with makeup. My parents and my husband begged me to stop, but my anxiety won every time. This is something else that I've been working on in therapy. It's getting better, but as I know now, it's a process.

Recently, I faced the biggest change of all when my husband and I moved to Germany for his first assignment with the U.S. Air Force.

My comfort zone was gone, my daily routine shattered to pieces. I was losing my family, my friends, the comfort of my house and my hometown, and my therapist.

I wish I could explain how I overcame the worst of my anxiety. There isn't one answer, at least not in my case. It took a long time for me to finally realize that I was simply tired of feeling the way I was feeling and that life was too short to worry this much. I was given this amazing opportunity, and while I had every right to feel anxious, I also knew I wanted to enjoy this experience as much as possible. Through hard work, lots of self-care, therapy, the endless support from my family, friends, and husband, as well as medication, I knew I was going to be okay.

Medication.

For a long time, I was ashamed, thinking about the idea of taking psychiatric medication. My therapist recommended it as a last resort, something to try if I felt that therapy wasn't fulfilling my needs. I was especially nervous that my family and friends would think that I was crazy for having to go on medication. Would I even be able to tell the difference after I started taking it, or would I just overthink it like everything else in my life? When the time came, and I finally decided I wanted to give medication a try, I thought to myself, *just give it a shot. What's the worst that could happen? If it doesn't work, then you'll stop taking medication.*

After trying it out for a few months, I started to notice small changes in my mood. I wasn't having as many racing thoughts, I wasn't freaking out as much over little things, and I was overall, a happier, calmer person. Medication for mental health isn't necessarily a cure-all, but it definitely helps me to tackle my anxiety. I'm no longer ashamed at having to take anxiety medication. My family and friends all know about it. They help to remind me to take it when my alarm goes off if I'm not standing right by my phone: "It's eight o'clock! Time to take your meds, Emily!" they shout across the house without hesitation or judgment in their tone. They know this is just a part of who I am. They don't see me any differently because of it.

Throughout my eating disorder, recovery, and struggles with anxiety, my family and friends have been there for me no matter what. That's not to say it was easy on them. I lost friends because my eating disorder made me isolated and cold. My parents weathered more pain and anger than I can put into words. My then-boyfriend/now husband stood by me at my worst.

What did I want from my loved ones? I wanted them to support me. When asked if I was okay, I would lie and say I was fine, too embarrassed or uncomfortable to explain how I was really feeling. I felt like my thoughts were silly and miniscule, that I was being immature and simply needed to grow up. I wanted understanding and love.

Mental health is confusing and everyone experiences things differently, but this is what I needed (and didn't need): I didn't need or expect them to know exactly what I was feeling or to understand every aspect of my anxiety, but rather to simply listen and understand I was struggling. I wanted validation for my feelings. I wanted them to know when I was angry at them, it was likely my anxiety rearing its ugly head, because if I was worrying about something, I often took it out on those closest to me. Every anxious thought I had, and my reaction to it, had nothing to do with them and everything to do with me. I wanted them to be patient with me. That was really all. I didn't need them to know everything about my anxiety. I didn't need them to take on the role of therapist or to instinctively know how to help me all of the time. I just needed them to be there…to understand.

For the rest of it, therapy and medication have been a huge help to me. Therapy helped me change my life. I've learned how to cope with my anxiety and how to give it the middle finger whenever I can. Do I still struggle with it? Hell yeah. But, through therapy I've learned that while there are some things that can be a catalyst for my anxiety (such as change), other times, it just hits me for no reason. Not only do my parents and my husband have a hard time understanding this, but sometimes I still do as well. Even so, therapy has helped me to accept it, to accept the lack of logic about what triggers my anxiety, and to stop regarding my "weakness" as the sole cause of my anxiety.

Every day is different. Some days, I'm incredibly anxious and don't know why; other days, I feel like I'm on top of the world, and I can accomplish anything. When I find myself stressing about food, focusing too much on exercise, or leaning towards the mirror to pick at my face, I'm able to pause and take a step back, thinking about the anxiety that I'm really feeling rather than masking it. Rather than trying to plan and control everything when I start feeling anxious, I have to be comfortable with letting the pieces fall where they may.

I don't believe I'll ever be fully "cured" of my anxiety, because as corny as it sounds, it isn't a destination, but a journey. Every day brings something different, and I've finally learned that rather than trying to control it, I simply have to *let go*. I might still worry incessantly, but my head is finally in the right place, and I'm making progress every day. The best I can do to control my anxiety right now is the best I can do right now. And that's okay.

For example, tonight, I'll get up off the couch, stretch my arms overhead, and yawn. 9:58. Time to go to bed. I'll walk to the bathroom thinking to myself the whole way, *don't look in the mirror.*

Even while telling myself this, I will be drawn in like a magnet, face up-close, so that I can see everything. On good days, I'm there for ten minutes. On bad days, sometimes more than an hour, picking and poking, sometimes bleeding. It'll probably be more like half an hour tonight.

I'll lie down next to him, the one who makes me feel better. I'll wrap my arm around his chest, settle my head into the crook of his neck, and take a deep breath. No matter how tired I am, I won't go to sleep right away. I can't.

My back will itch. I'll move to reach, scratch the itch, and then settle back against him. Then my foot. Move, scratch, settle. Then my arm. Move, scratch, settle. I'll feel the back of my leg and my forehead itch at the same time. Move, scratch, move, scratch, settle. I'll notice I'm clenching my jaw. I'll try to let go of the tension and take a deep breath. My foot will start tapping. My thoughts will keep racing.

I should probably start buying stuff for the bachelorette party. I need to buy shot glasses, a sash, lingerie, streamers, and alcohol. And I need to buy necklaces, snacks, and a banner. I must call the resort and make a dinner reservation. Shit, what if the room reservations never went through? Then the whole party will be ruined, and it'll be all my fault. What if no one has a good time because I'm not a good maid of honor?

I need to start my homework assignment for the week. It's already Wednesday. I should have started it today or yesterday. I'll do it tomorrow morning before driving to class. I'll set my alarm early.

But what if I'm too tired and don't get up? No, I'll set my alarm for 7:00, make tea, and eat a banana. Do the assignment from 7:30-8:30. Work out from 9:00 to 10:00. Get out of the shower by 10:30. Get ready till 11:00. Eat and make lunch for later. Leave by 12:30 the latest. Drive the two and a half hours to class. Eat lunch before class. Sit in class for three hours. Grab dinner, and then drive the two and a half hours back. Maybe I'll do some homework after I get back around 10:00....

I'll sigh, knowing that my day never goes as planned anyway. I'll wait for my mind to quiet enough to finally settle into an uneasy sleep.

And then I'll get up and do it all over again—as calmly as I can.

Jennifer: Walk it Off

The summer after I finished fifth grade, my parents planned a dream vacation. We were going to Florida to visit family and then spend 10 days between Disneyworld and Universal Studios. My ten-year-old brain couldn't even fathom the excitement I was feeling. But about a month before we left, I remember waking up during the night in cold sweats convinced that something awful was going to happen on the trip. I was certain something terrible was going to happen to one of my parents or to our dog, Roxie, whom I loved like a sibling. I just knew it. I conjured up plenty of terrible things. Every time I thought about the trip, my entire body filled with dread, and my stomach dropped to the floor like we were already on the first drop of Magic Mountain. I couldn't breathe from the adrenaline pumping through my veins. And there was no talking me out of it. Trust me, my parents tried.

The vacation went off without a hitch. Nothing bad happened. We had an amazing experience at Disney and once we were there, I managed to relax just a little bit more each day. But the anxiety that I started to feel before we left didn't end when we got back home. I didn't understand at the time, but I was having panic attacks—a fear of the uncontrollable, a fear of my loved ones suffering or dying, a certainty something bad was going to happen even though I couldn't explain why I felt this way, and I couldn't tell you what exactly was going to happen.

It grew and became increasingly catastrophic in nature as I got older. With age comes the ability to imagine increasingly more frightening things happening—things you didn't even know could happen a year ago. I think the world gets a little scarier for everyone with age and, on some level, that's normal. But this was beyond that. Every new thing I learned about was a potential danger from which I had to protect myself. I was constantly on high alert. And nothing was scarier than the dangers I couldn't see. Germs. Bacteria. Viruses. Tiny things I couldn't see but that could kill me in an instant, before I even knew they were there. My mind understood certain people, places, and situations exposed me to higher levels of bacteria than others, but I developed a compulsion to wash, clean, and sanitize until I felt everything was safe.

This was before hand sanitizer was popular. Although that may have made my daily routines a lot faster, it wouldn't have stopped them. The rational part of my mind was no longer in control. If rather than washing my hands for five minutes, all I had to do was wipe a squirt of hand sanitizer on my hands, why would I limit myself to only cleaning my hands before I ate, before I touched my face, and when I came into and out of my house? I could clean them after I touched anything that didn't belong to me. The one thing I did know was that the more I could control, the better I felt.

This need for control and this need to manage what I saw as the major risks in my environment grew into germ phobia and a diagnosis of obsessive-compulsive disorder while I was still a teenager. But it didn't stop there. The hits kept coming. And my anxiety, never one to be defeated, hit back harder every time.

My dad was deployed after 9/11 to fight another invisible enemy…one that I'd never seen and rarely even heard about but had already caused an incredible tragedy and an incomprehensible amount of loss less than 100 miles from my home. What was to stop them from doing it again? What else didn't we see coming?

At thirteen, my best friend committed suicide. I didn't see that coming. In my junior year of high school, five of my friends died in two separate fatal car crashes…suddenly and without warning. On the same road…one we drove on every day. Then my grandparents passed away. So did my aunts and uncles.

I can't honestly say everything that happened during my middle and high school years was horrible or scary. It wasn't. Maybe the tragedies look worse condensed like this, when they're focused on after the fact, when I'm only telling you the bad parts. But for me, this was the stuff I focused on. I thought about it all the time. How could I not? Even setting aside my personal pain at the loss of people I loved, the fact that the world was incredibly dangerous was more apparent every passing year. Hidden dangers lurked everywhere.

The panic attacks returned with a vengeance; shaking, sweating, nausea, heart racing, stomach pain, difficulty breathing. My mind took over and caused catastrophic effects on my body. I had no control over my body or my thoughts. If my mother was late getting home from work, I would leap to thinking she had been in a car accident and was therefore, in a ditch somewhere. When my then-boyfriend didn't pick up his phone, I would assume he was also in said ditch. My loved ones catered to my fears. I remember asking my boyfriend to text me after he moved his truck from his driveway to his grandparents' driveway, literally thirty feet away from his. He did. It didn't hurt anyone, and it made me feel better. What was the harm?

My mother, a therapist, worked with me and desperately tried to get me the help that I needed, which included therapy and psychotropic medication. However, in retrospect, I think the most important thing she did was to make sure I never feared the stigma of asking for help. Despite the incredible pain she must have been in trying to help me with no end to the struggle in sight, she did everything she could to reassure me that it was all going to be okay, that there were plenty of other people out there like me, and that it could and would get better. I credit her entirely for where I am today and for helping me gain the skills to keep my head above water.

My father also provided a surprising strategy that has helped me immensely. I'm not sure if it's something he passed along to me because he noticed it was something that helps him or if he's had more exposure to panic attacks and PTSD then I give him credit for during his time overseas. Regardless, despite how counterintuitive it can feel at times, it still works for me.

He was with me when I was having a panic attack in high school…a bad one. A coworker and high school classmate had failed to show up for our shift that morning. So, I was already in panic mode. We eventually found out that my classmate had, in fact, died in a car accident the night before. I immediately fell off the edge of the cliff I had been clinging to while we waited. I knew I should do whatever I could to remain calm. I had been trying. In an instant, my body was already betraying me. My heart was pounding so fast, I was sure it would never stop. I couldn't catch my breath. I was pretty sure I never would. This was how I was going to die. My father told me to go for a walk. I couldn't. My legs were jelly. I couldn't breathe for Christ's sake. I couldn't think of a single thing that I could do that would make less sense than going for a walk. I also couldn't really process information enough to think at all, and he repeated, over and over again, loudly enough that I could hear it, over the hub of noise in my head, but very calmly, "Jen, go for a walk," until I finally heard him. So, I walked…for hours.

My blood flow was gradually redirected from my heart and digestive system to my limbs. I felt more in control. I was still out of breath. My heart was still racing. But that was because I was speed walking, not for some unknown reason that certainly signaled I was in imminent danger. When I finally slowed my pace hours later, my heart slowed as well. My breathing came back to normal. I was okay.

I'm not saying this is the solution for everyone, or all of the time. But sometimes if I can redirect that physical "fight or flight" sensation from that initial burst of adrenaline into a physical sensation that makes sense to me, I can get ahead of it. If I can say over and over to myself "your heart is racing because you are exercising" and not "your heart is racing because something horrible is about to happen" or "your heart is racing because it's failing and you are about to die," I can trick my mind into calming. If my heart is racing because I'm power walking, if I stop walking, logically, my heart should stop racing. Sometimes it does.

The panic attacks have lessened somewhat since I graduated from college, met my husband, and gave birth to my daughter (being a mom gives way to a never-ending stream of new worries). I think some of what has helped me manage the panic attacks has been time. And, sadly, repetition. I still have them. Still, despite some of my early panic attacks happening at the same time that real tragedy had struck without warning, hundreds of others since then have come and passed without major catastrophe. The more likely scenario is undoubtedly that my mind is playing with me right now, not that my world is about to come crashing down, yet again.

It is an ever-present struggle. Even when I lose that battle and feel the physical symptoms of an attack, I remind myself over and over again that I know why I'm feeling what I'm feeling, that it's not rational, and it's not going to kill me. At least, it hasn't yet. There are times I've been more afraid, that my heart was going faster than this, times when I've had better reasons to be afraid than I do right now. And I'm still here. At the end of the day, fear can't actually kill you. It just makes you think it can.

James: The Anxiety Monster

"To my family and friends that have accepted
me for me, laughed with me, cried with me, and helped
me when there was a need, and proven to me that there are indeed
flowers to be found in the world that at times seems to
be full of weeds, I say thank you. I love you,
and you mean the world to me."
—*Mountain Wisdom*

I had a great childhood; I had two loving parents who always showed up to support every single thing that I ever did or accomplished. They did everything they could to ensure my childhood was as perfect as possible. I had a lot of friends, and I was even one of the popular kids in elementary school. Then puberty hit, and everything changed. I became shy and awkward. I developed a severe case of social anxiety. I never wanted to talk because I felt like everyone was judging me. Even around my family, I was extremely quiet. I reasoned that they would be in my life forever, and I did not want to risk embarrassing myself around them or take the chance of saying anything that would result in them not liking me for the rest of my life.

My sense of self-worth and confidence vanished along with my childhood as I got older. I grew my hair long into an ugly bowl cut in an attempt to hide from the world. I developed severe acne all over my face and body. I still have the scars from it today. I had every problem possible with my jaw and teeth: braces, an expander, a Herbst device, and a metal guard that goes around the outside of your mouth. In middle school, I had to get Botox shots in my armpits because my hyperhidrosis was so intense; the prescription-strength deodorant burned my armpits so badly that I could not sleep. I was growing so quickly that my mom bought my clothing a size or two bigger because I outgrew everything so fast. By sixth grade, I was six feet tall. I never felt my clothes actually fit me. I weighed 145 pounds when I started lifting weights in high school. I currently weigh 224 pounds, and a few of the tee shirts still fit. Basically, I hated everything about my appearance, and the kids at school destroyed any shred of confidence that I might have had left. It started in fourth grade when two girls, who I thought were my best friends, logged onto my AOL account and spread the rumor that I was gay and in love with my best friend. The bullying started and never really ended until I graduated.

I never stood up for myself, not even once. I was afraid of what the kids would say or do if I did. I did not want to make the situation any worse. I avoided being the center of attention, so I definitely never wanted to get into a physical altercation and have everyone standing around me, watching the outcome, and talking about it afterwards. I hated presentations that required me to stand up in front of the class and talk for this same reason. I did not like walking into anywhere late or leaving early because I just knew everyone was going to look at me and judge me. I hated being singled out in front of other people, even if it was to receive an award. I would rather sit in the crowd unrecognized for my achievements. I hated school projects requiring a partner because I was worried about being the one kid who did not get chosen to be a partner. This worry was validated because it happened on multiple occasions. I allowed all of these doubts and fears to affect my inner psyche and thoughts. My social anxiety grew boundlessly until it consumed me. It got to the point where I could not even order food at a fast food restaurant or go buy something from a gas station because of my fear of social interaction. My friends and family enabled this behavior by ordering for me, so I didn't have to force myself to get over it. This is just one example of how my life was impacted by my social anxiety. The fear of social interaction seeped into every aspect of my life.

Around the age of fourteen, I began to drink in excess and blacked out often. Alcohol helped diminish my negative thoughts and feelings of not being good enough. It seemed to be the only way to put the anxiety monster to sleep for a little while. It allowed me to be more social without as much fear of being judged. It seemed like a reasonable coping intervention since so many adults I knew drank alcohol and lived normal lives. I thought that it was such a good idea to calm my anxiety that I poured five shots into my blender bottle before my communications presentation my freshman year of college. I hoped it would increase my confidence and decrease the amount of nervousness that I had standing in front of the entire class. Honestly in that situation, five shots weren't enough because I was equally as nervous as sober James would have been.

By college, I had already fallen in love with lifting weights. I was, or should I say wanted to be, an athlete my entire life. I played basketball in my youth, but I was never particularly good at it. I gave it my all and tried, but the natural talent was just not there. Although I made one of the best AAU teams in my area, I did not even make the varsity team when I was a junior in high school. It still doesn't make much sense to me. Even though I wasn't great at basketball, I enjoyed physical activity. The day I got my driver's license I started going to the gym every day.

Building muscle was one aspect of my physical appearance that I could change and improve upon. I worked out every day for hours and made friends through the journey of my physical transformation. I became one of the biggest, most muscular guys in my college gym during my senior year. Working out definitely helped with my stress levels, confidence, and anxiety.

Even sometimes when I walk into the gym, the place where I feel the most comfortable and the best about myself, someone can glance at me or laugh with their friend, and I automatically feel judged and inadequate. Then all that I can think about for the rest of my workout is, "What is wrong with me? Why did they laugh at me?" One time a few years ago, my friend was at the gym with her friend, and they were looking at me, pointing, and giggling. It made me feel so self-conscious. I was upset and felt betrayed because she was my friend and even she was making fun of me. Days later, I talked to my friend about that situation, and I was shocked to find out that they were talking about how good I looked. Unfortunately, my brain goes straight to telling me that people are always thinking negatively about me and that I am not good enough.

Thinking about my future freaks me out. I imagine most people think about their future. After all, it is smart to plan ahead and have goals. However, I overthink it to the point of becoming fixated on every possible way that I can fail. I struggle to feel successful because even when I accomplish something, it doesn't feel like enough. I always feel like I need to catch up or like I am failing at life. I have accomplished a few things since graduating high school; I graduated college with honors, I currently hold the Virginia state record in powerlifting in my weight class, I won my first bodybuilding show, I got one of a limited number of Graduate Assistant positions at a reputable master's program, I moved down south by myself and made all new friends, I have my own apartment, and I got accepted into the second best physical therapy program in the nation. I am sure there is more, but the point and the problem remains the same. I still feel like I have not accomplished a single thing in my life truly worthy of being proud of or celebrating. I wish that I could feel a sense of accomplishment and pride for myself.

I just keep thinking that I have not achieved enough in life, and that I am falling behind of my peers and my personal timeline. I am not where I should be by now. I thought I would be an independent, accomplished adult by the age of 25, and I have not even started down my desired career path yet.

Twenty-five feels pretty old. I was sure by now I would at least be engaged, if not married, to the girl of my dreams. I really want to be in a long-term relationship. I want to get married. I want the security of knowing I will always have that one, special person by my side who loves me and accepts me. In all my past relationships, I have obsessed over not knowing where the relationship will go. I worried I would make a mistake, no matter how small and lose her. I worried that I would be left for someone better than me. And if she leaves me, I fear I will never find a woman who makes me happier than she made me. My anxiety about being alone is consuming and frightening. I have a great deal of love to give and feel I need to find that special someone for me. Time is running out according to my life plan.

My lack of confidence and self-worth flows through all areas of my life, but I am working on changing this. I am focused on my self-development and on building new coping strategies. The gym was my only outlet for stress and my only coping mechanism, but it also turned into a new addiction. I needed to work out every day, and if I could not make it to the gym, I would get more stressed out. It did not matter what was going on in my life…I had to go to the gym. Holidays, vacations, long workdays, and hung-over mornings were no exception to this obsession. All of a sudden, the coronavirus pandemic hit America, and every gym in the country closed overnight. I felt like I had lost my entire life; ten years of hard work in the gym, the highlight of my day, my coping mechanism, and my next bodybuilding show that I was prepping for were about to go to waste. I could not maintain my muscle mass and I lost 20 pounds in just weeks. As my body shrunk and my shirts were not as tight, I physically felt all my progress melting away. I cannot explain the impact this had on my life and mental health. When you squat 500 pounds in the gym, it is difficult to create a workout with a similar intensity at home. Actually, more like impossible. Sure, I could walk, run, do sit ups, pull ups. I did 1,500 push-ups in one workout and 750 pull-ups in another at the park, but it was not the same.

I was forced to find other ways to manage my anxiety. I went to see a psychiatrist. I think the medicine he put me on is helping. I discovered listening to self-motivational audio books helps me stay in a more positive place and learn about how and why people think and feel certain thoughts and emotions. I started seeing a therapist after reading the book *Maybe You Should Talk to Someone* by Lori Gottlieb. My therapist has helped me more than I ever imagined was possible. I really did not believe much in therapy until I met her. But I was wrong, and I highly recommend trying it. I have started regaining control of my anxiety with all of these added modalities.

However, the best thing that I ever did for my anxiety was adopting my dog. I rescued Thor six years ago from a shelter when he was a puppy. Thor gave me a purpose and a reason to live when I felt like I no longer had one. He loves me just the way that I am. No one will ever get as excited to see me when I come home as he does. We go on walks, hikes, to the dog park, and the beach. He sleeps by my side every night. He is reliant on me for food, protection, and love. I make sure he is always happy and feeling loved and appreciated, and he does the same for me.

Even with all of this progress, my anxiety is still present. It is with me in every thought I have throughout every day. I am making progress in controlling my negative thoughts about myself and my fear of the future. My life would be so different if I could stop worrying and judging myself. I am looking for the positive in every situation and in myself. I am grateful for those moments and experiences where I get to feel confident and at peace with the world. These tiny glimpses into how it could feel gives me hope. I understand the years after college graduation are stressful and lonely as you search deep within yourself for who and what you are going to be in life. You also have to figure out where to live, where to work, how to make new friends, how to make your mark on the world while being happy in the process, and hopefully finding the love of your life and starting a family. Life is full of difficult decisions and requires you to face the unknown. Any wonder why I am so anxious?

Zack: Me, My Mother and I

I've been struggling with anxiety, in some form or another, for as long as I can remember. When I was younger, it tended to be random and small things that sparked my worry. I would worry something would go wrong or something bad would happen on a trip to the movies or the zoo. It was odd and somewhat distressing to me, but it didn't stop me from being able to do things and live my life. As I grew, so did the severity of the thoughts. By the time I was in high school, they consumed me.

As I entered tenth grade, a crippling fear of something bad happening to Mom while I was at school grabbed onto me and refused to let go. I still don't know where this life-changing fear came from, why it chose that time in my life, or how it got to the point where I couldn't make it leave me alone. Nothing bad had happened. My mom had one health scare when I was a kid, but that was ten years prior to this and wasn't something I'd given any conscious thought to since then. I just woke up one morning, and the fear was there… taunting me.

I worried all day every day that something awful was going to happen to her. I was sure she was going to suffer a random heart attack, be in a car accident, or an intruder would break into the house and hurt her. I was terrified she was going to die, and I felt this panic as intensely as if I had just been told by the police that it had actually happened. My entire mind and body responded to this thought as if it were real.

The only way I could confirm she was still alive and safe was to call her. So, I called her. My fear sprang to life each morning, even before the homeroom bell rang. As soon as I arrived at school and got off the bus, I would call my mom before I headed into school. As hard as I tried, I only pulled off that I was talking to a friend each morning for a while before a bunch of the other students realized I was talking to my mom every morning. As embarrassing as this was, I had to do it. It wasn't a choice. I called her in between most of my classes. This required me to go to the third-floor bathroom and stand close to the window to get reception. It was one of the only places I had cell service and only a small chance of getting caught. Talking to her and hearing her voice was the only way to pause the fear and buy myself a few minutes of knowing that she was okay.

Some mornings the fear was so overwhelming I would intentionally miss the bus so my mom had to drive me to school. This way, I knew for just a little longer she was safe. I could see her. Some days, this would help; other days, it fueled my anxiety more. I would get out of the car at school, and it would hit me that I was putting my mother's life in unnecessary jeopardy by having her drive me. While she was driving home from dropping me off at school, there was an even higher chance that she could die in a car accident. I should have taken the bus and left her at home, safe. Then I felt guilty and selfish. She would reassure me as soon as possible upon arriving home by leaving me a voice message that she was home and safe. God forbid she got stuck in traffic and it took her a few extra minutes to get home, this would put me into a full-fledged panic.

Eventually my anxiety escalated to the point that I was terrified to go to school at all. I had constant panic attacks every time I thought about it and I just couldn't stay calm enough to actually get to school. We eventually spoke with my school guidance counselor and asked for help and support. He was helpful at first, and we developed a plan to have my mom come to school and spend the day in the office. This way I would have peace of mind knowing she was in the building and safe. Obviously, this was a temporary solution for a few days to see if it helped. It did help, as I was able to concentrate at school and experienced less panic.

The last day Mom was going to stay at the school, we were in the guidance counselor's office in the morning, and he asked to speak with us. He told us I had proven I could get through the day without worrying and having to talk to my mom, and he believed this proved I would now be fine. He told my mom to leave. She was hesitant, but he said it was for my own good. He was the professional, so she got up and left. My anxiety came rushing back, and I struggled to follow her. My guidance counselor grabbed me and physically held me back so that I couldn't go with her. All I could do was stand there and watch her leave and imagine all the ways she was in danger. I was completely devastated, I felt helpless and betrayed by him. I had believed I could trust him. I sat there in his office in tears. All I could do was wait to get a call from my mom when she got home, and I did, after what felt like an eternity. I managed to get through the day, feeling anxious and depressed.

It was at this point, on that day, I felt like I had hit rock bottom. I lost all motivation to do anything; I was always anxious and/or depressed. I was afraid I was actually going crazy. I didn't think there was any hope or that anything could be done to help me. My parents took me to the doctor, who referred me to a psychiatrist and therapist. I was prescribed antidepressants, which helped me tremendously. At the time, I was embarrassed that I needed to be medicated. But it helped me. I still had some of the fears, but they were less intense…more tolerable. I was better able to reason through these fears after some of the raw emotion subsided.

I now realize how common it is to take medication for anxiety. Around this time, I read articles in magazines about a few musicians I respected and looked up to because I was a big fan. In one of those articles, I read several of the band members had anxiety and struggled with similar issues I was facing. These musicians also took antidepressants, and this helped me realize that I wasn't alone. I have since discovered there is a history of mental illness in my family and so, even within my family, I'm not alone in this regard.

I've started to understand, accept, and gain insight that needing medical help doesn't make me any less than anyone else. It doesn't make me weak. It's mostly a function of brain wiring, not determination. There is nothing wrong with taking medication or seeking a clinical professional to talk with about your worries. I'm very encouraged to see the progress in mental health awareness in just over a decade since I sought help for the first time, but there's still a long way to go for both society and myself. It was important for me to share my story because I know personally how important it is if you are struggling with a mental illness to know you aren't alone. Talk to and accept help from the people who care about you. Let them in. Sharing your thoughts and fears and engaging in treatment for your mental health isn't a weakness. It takes strength and courage. I am going to be a dad soon, and I plan to share this message with my daughter and raise her to understand mental health is just as important as physical health.

I really can't wait to meet her!

Faith: Oh, That Anxiety Feeling

I don't remember a time in my life where I did not have "that" feeling in my chest. You know, *that* feeling. The one where your entire chest is tight, your heart feels like it's petrifying with each beat, and breathing becomes so difficult you are convinced you are going to drown on dry land. That feeling.

As an adult, I now know what that feeling is—anxiety. It is perpetual nervousness and fear that runs on a movie reel like a horror movie over and over again until you have all the lines memorized, only to find out that someone, something, went behind your back and changed the script. Then it starts all over again. A lot of people can tell you how anxiety exists in their world. Whether growing up with it as I did or experiencing an event that triggers anxiety going forward, anxiety exists in so many people and manifests in many different ways.

I can identify concrete things in my life that contributed to my anxiety, some of which I still have residual effects from to this day. As a child, I experienced abuse and violence that impacts me as an adult. I experience trepidation and fear around large men and in crowds. I experience panic attacks when I think I may be in trouble over something. I have to ask my bosses not to send me emails or text messages that ask me to see them when I get into work because I get physically ill over wondering what is wrong.

But often, my anxiety is more nebulous and has less of a clear cause or logic behind it. It can be hard to identify. When I was little, I was afraid of our house burning down. I still check the outlets and make sure everything is unplugged when I leave my apartment. I have a large keychain because my uncle told me my keys could be a weapon, and now I can't have a small set of keys without feeling unprotected. I panic, thinking the absolute worst has happened if a friend is a few minutes late meeting me or picking me up. As a paramedic, I spent hours logging inventories of every ambulance and jump bag, to make sure everything was where it was supposed to be. I would line up my intubation kits on the counter whenever I had a call that caused that feeling…just in case. I always answer work calls because what if I did something wrong and my job needed me to fix it? Or what if I actually failed, the college made a mistake, and I wasn't qualified to be a paramedic anymore? When my boss would email or text me that she needed to talk to me, I would panic. What if my patient died because of something I did? What if I put the wrong tool in the wrong pocket? Did I misuse the computer at work looking up extra training courses? What did I do wrong? What if, what if, what if, what if….

My anxiety is cruel and unyielding. It incites deep-seated issues of shame and unworthiness that feed into suicidal thoughts, violent ruminations, and severe depression. It wasn't my fault I experienced violence and cruelty as a small child. It wasn't my fault my father would never show up, leaving me to sit at a window for hours wondering what I did wrong. It isn't my fault for experiencing shame, or guilt, or fear. Nor is it my fault my anxiety triggers symptoms related to PTSD, bipolar disorder, or OCD. But anxiety makes me feel like it is my fault, that I should have control, and I am somehow weaker, or lesser, for not being able to control my anxiety.

Yet, as I said, I don't remember a time in my life when I didn't feel anxiety. My early years were filled with this feeling that I thought was just…normal. It was as normal as the violence, anger, and cruelty I experienced in my world. It was as normal as the death threats and bullying I experienced at the schools I was in. According to my therapist, my experiences with anxiety were normal responses to trauma. Normal, normal, normal. The tightness in my chest, the inability to breathe, my heart feeling like it was turning into stone—all apparently normal. *Normal?* Really?

Personally, I don't believe in normal. Looking back at everything I have been through, and everything I am still going through, nothing is normal, and the ever-present anxiety still finds its way in through the cracks in the foundation of my life. I always had this picture of what I wanted my life to be like. I wanted to be married, have kids, work a great job, and live so far from New York that I would have to take out a world map to point to it. I worked my entire life towards this vision and suffered from severe anxiety and other mental-health symptoms whenever it appeared my life was deviating from this vision. It didn't matter that I was diagnosed with bipolar disorder when I was in college. It didn't matter that I developed obsessive-compulsive habits stemming from anxiety linked to the abuse from my childhood. It didn't matter that my anxieties triggered deep, unchecked depressions and suicidal ideations. It didn't matter that I had already attempted suicide twice before the age of twenty-two. I just believed it would all simply go away once I achieved this life I believed I should be living. I didn't listen to my mind, nor my body, as my anxiety grew and escalated further out of control.

In 2012, I met my ex-wife and fell completely head-over-heels. I was living in Iowa at the time and was trying to rebuild my life after spending almost a year crippled by feelings of failure and unworthiness. I met my wife, and I felt much of the tension in my world start to ease. We married in 2014, in the middle of me achieving my associate degree in emergency medicine, and I felt untouchable. I had a job that I felt was worthwhile, and I was married to someone I thought was the one for me. However, I still experienced anxiety on a regular basis. I couldn't go to sleep without checking to make sure all the doors and windows were locked three or four times, much to my wife's frustration at times. But it was okay.

Yet things were not as okay as I thought they were. I didn't realize until it was too late, "that feeling" that was still gripping my chest and only seemed to be getting worse. I would get sudden panic attacks at the thought of failing as a paramedic. Suddenly, it seemed the idea of having children was impossible. Thoughts of being a horrible parent, the anxiety of carrying a child, of being responsible like that, choked all the air out of my lungs. Growing cracks in my relationship fed the feeling in my chest and left me feeling like I was going 1,000 miles per hour with no one driving the car. I tried to ignore it. I began to drink myself to sleep regularly and pushed my body beyond its limits. My wife and I decided to move to Oregon early in our relationship…a horrifically bad idea.

I couldn't explain what I was feeling to anyone. I felt terrible and worthless all the time. My ability to handle work stresses started to wane. I was experiencing bullying and harassment at my job, and I began faltering in my ability to cope. Coupled with the anxiety of moving to Oregon with my wife, who was becoming more distant, the increased stress left me gasping for air in random parking lots in my car. I believed following my wife to Oregon, even though everything in me screamed "No!" would help. I quit my job, continued to drink, and struggled not to drown under the weight of my thoughts and feelings. The anxiety of failing in life raged against the growing anxiety of an increasingly abusive situation. I was trapped in the crossfire.

It came to a head in the spring of 2016, when everything just collapsed. I was thousands of miles away from my support system, surrounded by people who had no concern regarding my welfare and working a job that meant nothing. It was a nightmare. My anxiety levels were so high, I was physically ill every day and experiencing severe heart and stomach issues. I was isolated, running on alcohol and depression until I finally snapped. The anxiety of being in a toxic relationship and feeling like I deserved how I was being treated made me feel pathetic. It was killing me, and I felt myself crumbling. So, I called my family in New York and a few friends in Iowa, packed my car with everything I could fit in it, and drove away.

I spent two and a half days driving across the country trying to figure out how my life derailed so violently. How did I end up loving someone so blindly that I didn't see the abuse until it was too late? How did I let myself be manipulated and lied to? How did I end up so far away from help that I had to drive almost 3,000 miles just to see a friendly face? What did I do to deserve this? Something must be so horribly wrong with me to warrant all this pain. My depression and the end of my marriage must ultimately be my fault because something was wrong with me.

It took me three years to understand and accept that something wasn't wrong with me. To work through the pain of everything I had experienced throughout my life and not succumb to the crippling tightness that filled my chest whenever my anxiety overwhelmed me demonstrated strength. I still struggle with anxiety and panic attacks, although now I have a better understanding of what I am going through, and why I am going through it. Anxiety is like that… irrational and rational all at the same time. Anxiety still fills me with shame and fear. It still prevents me from sleeping. It makes me late for work and appointments. Anxiety forces me to check that my door is locked, even though I just locked it. However, it no longer feels like a death sentence.

Anxiety will forever play a huge role in my mental-health recovery. This knowledge actually brings me peace, if you can believe it. I understand its origins in my life, how it manifests, and have worked hard to build up my skills in coping with attacks. Recently, I was able to share with someone that I was experiencing a panic attack, and explain I just needed a moment. Maybe not in so many words, but they understood what I meant. I was then able to ground myself back into reality, tell myself I was safe, and allow my body to release the tension that had built up so suddenly that it surprised me. Because while I may have developed skills to deal with my anxiety and ask for help, the anxiety can still catch me off guard. It holds a lifetime pass to constrict my chest, roar in my ears, fog my mind, and surprise the hell out of me.

It isn't something to be ashamed about—not anymore. I take my anti-anxiety medications, work hard on my mental-health recovery, and am open about my struggles with anxiety. I still get mad when I have anxiety attacks, and there are days where I yell and cry. This is okay though. It is okay because I realize I am human. I am complex and simple and utterly flawed. In reality, having anxiety isn't one of those flaws. It just is, and after everything I've been through, I am okay with that. If you have anxiety, I hope you are, too.

Sam: Liar, Liar, My Mind is on Fire

My earliest memories revolve around elaborate stories I made up in my mind as a child. I would act them out. A stick and a rock would turn into a flying saucer hurtling through space and a ship that harbored a race of alien geniuses. I would reenact a battle between the aliens. These reenactments were intense, and I would forget what was going on around me. In reality, my parents were watching me bash a stick and a rock together while making tiny explosion noises. Normal kid stuff, right?

This behavior was initially attributed to my active imagination. Being lost in my own thoughts occasionally led to issues in the real world, but I was still a little kid. That was normal too, right? Kids are weird.

It wasn't until my little brothers were born that my parents started to realize I had significant interpersonal issues which "an active imagination" didn't entirely account for. When my brothers were born, I remember being overjoyed to meet them. However, I continued to believe the world ran according to my rules.

My little brother, Ben, would try to play with my action figures with me while I was enacting one of my glorious battle scenes. In order to play with me, Ben had to say the exact lines I had in my head and do the exact actions with the toys that I expected. He needed to know what I was thinking. So, obviously, when he pretended his characters were doing something that didn't align perfectly with the story inside my head, I flipped out on him and refused to continue playing. I retreated to a corner to act out the rest of my scene by myself.

The same issues arose when my youngest brother, Jake, was born. Eventually I learned to compromise while playing with my brothers, but it was very difficult for me to break from my fictional world. I was in control there, and I needed and liked it that way. I think if I had been an only child, I would have sunk deeper into myself and would be less functional today.

I also went through many obsessions as a child. I had eight "insect collections" from when I was passionate about capturing insects. Then came my obsession with "dragonology," an informative book series that convinced me dragons had once existed.

Oh, and I still have over one hundred hand-made comic books from when I became obsessed with writing a comic series about a superhero named Lizarndo. A friend and I also created a card game that was a total rip-off of Pokémon cards. We called them Exomon cards. These obsessions were always one at a time and became my sole focus. All my effort went into that one thing.

I've buried the lead a bit. I'm sure at least some people reading this already know what this all adds up to in terms of diagnosis. According to my parents, I was diagnosed with Asperger's Syndrome at the age of four. I was unable to transition from one activity to another, and when forced to do so, would have uncontrollable meltdowns, triggering my parents to have me tested. It was determined that I had Asperger's Syndrome, also known as high-functioning autism.

I was an eccentric kid in elementary school. No getting around it. I've already told you about the comic books. And the insects. And the dragons. Add to all of that, I had a rather theatrical personality, and my obsession with my own imagination was at a peak. You can start to get the picture.

Still, I remember those elementary years being void of any anxiety or self-consciousness. It wasn't until later, when I first experienced the unrestrained judgment of the kids in the middle school cafeteria, that my social anxiety was ignited.

I went from a small elementary school full of familiar faces and friends to a conglomeration of five separate schools all merged into one middle school. I tried sticking to the familiar friends I knew from elementary school. It wasn't long before they told me that I wasn't cool enough to sit at their lunch table.

The entire concept of categories of people and popularity was a foreign concept to me. Some of this was Asperger's, I'm sure. The idea of classifying humans like I used to classify bugs, however, had never occurred to me. It still doesn't make sense to me. People are people. They have differences, sure. But not really classifiable ones unless you start going by hair color, skin color, or size, like you would bugs. And although I wasn't sure of much when it came to this popularity thing, this did not seem to be the system they were going by.

Just like that, I was left not only without a place to sit at lunch, but confused as to why I, in particular, was especially uncool. I tried twenty different ways, but I could not understand what it was that determined someone's popularity. I eventually came to the only logical conclusion. Something was wrong with me. I blamed myself.

Over time, I became cautious and stopped talking to people for fear that I was being judged. This fear grew and took over. I began to tell myself everyone was constantly judging me. I told myself I was an awful and awkward person and that everyone around me secretly hated me. I told myself they talked shit about me behind my back.

I never found a clique where I belonged in high school either. I floated from one group of friends to the other looking to be accepted, but most of the time, I was locked in my room creating music. My focus shifted entirely to music. My social interactions consisted of people I was making music with, either in a band or performing in theater.

Even academically I struggled a bit. I found myself getting into arguments with teachers who thought their subject was more important than music. I made it very clear to everyone that I had already chosen a path for my life. I had great relationships with the teachers in charge of music and theater as well as some teachers who found a way to get along with a somewhat sulky 15-year old who made it very clear that nothing had ever, or would ever, matter to his life if it wasn't related to music. Not everyone found that particular trait endearing.

I made it to college without major incident. Still, I was unhappy overall with how high school had gone for me, and I attributed this to a lack of social connections. I resolved not to make the same mistakes again. In college, I would abandon my "hermit music guy" reputation. I would try to become someone cooler. Someone whom people wanted to hang out with. I would finally experience all that life had to offer.

There is one time-tested way to ease anxiety in social situations (especially uncomfortable ones with people you don't know at all) and feel like you're having a great time: alcohol. Add to this, I was determined to never again turn down a new experience out of fear, which of course, led to some casual drug use, and you get a pretty good sense of my freshman year.

There were good things that happened. I met some of the coolest and most eccentric people who are still my friends today. I was humbled and hit hard by the incredible musical talent that surrounded me on campus. My ego and any confidence I had developed about my musical ability was crushed. It upset and concerned me. By sophomore year, I channeled this anxiety about how I stacked up with my new friends musically into a renewed sense of focus on my education and career in the music industry.

Schoolwork, music projects, and classes now took up most of my time. I lived with two roommates off campus. One of them had issues of his own that he was dealing with, but his unpredictability and sudden swings of anger contributed to stress in our home that was toxic for me. I became increasingly depressed and anxious. Panic attacks and meltdowns became frequent and overwhelming.

By senior year, I'd found a new living situation and a new method of dealing with depression and anxiety: distraction. I started a new band, opened a DIY venue in the garage of my new place, and recorded an incredibly ambitious final project. Altogether, I managed to get my anxiety back down to a tolerable level.

Today, I'm happier overall. I still struggle with depression and anxiety. You can see my autism in brief flashes. I control my behavior to the point most people I meet today are surprised to hear I am on the spectrum, but the social anxiety that began to grow within me in middle school has never left. To this day, the same negative thoughts creep into my head every time I meet someone new. *I'm acting weird. I'm coming off as dumb.* My thoughts play out the worst-case scenario for every situation. And although I know these thoughts, too loud to ignore, are really just my brain trying to trick me, they're still powerful enough to convince me otherwise. What if they're right this time?

I have been prescribed medicine for my social anxiety, but I also tend to heavily self-medicate with marijuana. I still have occasional panic attacks. Sometimes they'll hit me out of nowhere in a social setting. Suddenly, it feels like everyone is giving me a weird look like I've just pissed on myself, and my chest begins to feel heavy from the intensity of the stares. I can't help but immediately conclude I'm acting bizarre and everyone is judging me.

The pressure of this self-imposed delusion makes it impossible for me to form a thought or sentence, so I don't say anything, even when spoken to. I've taught myself how to react when I have these attacks, which basically boils down to getting the hell out of the situation. Once I've gotten away from people, I have my meltdown in private and wait until the attack passes.

None of it bothers me as much as it used to. I've been getting better at ignoring the voice in my head that reminds me how terrible I am all of the time, how awkward I am, why everyone is looking at me *like that*. Maybe the voice will never shut up, and it will always be there berating me with insults and worst-case scenarios, but at least I am able to convince myself that everything it is saying is bullshit… most of the time.

It's harder than you would think to call your own brain a liar and actually believe it. It's difficult to convince myself that these negative thoughts in my head are lies because the thoughts are coming from me. And the thoughts telling me not to believe the negative thoughts are also coming from my brain. So, clearly my brain is, at best, confused.

Rachel: The Good Girl

When I was a little girl, my parents told me to make sure nothing touched the electrical outlets, because it could start a fire. Being the dutiful daughter, I didn't allow anything to touch the outlets in my room except electrical cords. They said this once or twice. It wasn't something that kept them up at night. Being the anxious child I was, I'd lie awake in worry, getting up every few minutes to turn on the lights and check the outlets. There was no magic number of times I had to check. I would just check, and check, and check, and check, until I was too tired to worry and check anymore. I never thought there was anything wrong with this. I was being a good girl. I was preventing a fire.

I was always a worrier. Most often, I was worried about getting into trouble. I worried about being good and not doing anything wrong. I didn't have any traumatic experience to make me worry about punishment. I wasn't abused, and although my mom was a yeller, she got over things with remarkable speed and ultimately ended up apologizing to my brothers and me for getting angry. I honestly can't tell you why I worried like I did. Or why I continue to worry like this. I just do.

When I think of my worrying tendencies in my teen years, I think about my high school boyfriend. He was my neighbor, and we spent every spare moment together. We had a lot of fun together and loved each other deeply (at least that's how it felt at the time). Our biggest challenge was my worrying; specifically, my worrying about us getting in trouble. He was much more adventurous and enjoyed taking the risks that teenagers love to take. This would cause me to get angry with him for fear of getting caught. I'd yell, nag, and just constantly be angry with him because he was "going to get us into trouble." Then I'd worry he was going to break up with me, and I'd sob uncontrollably. Some of this was teen angst and raging hormones. Most of it was just my worrying stopping me from being able to do anything else.

My boyfriend and I spent most of our time with his friends because they all lived in the neighborhood. However, one night during Christmas break, we went out with my friend group. My mom told me I could stay out past curfew, but not too late. Those were really the only guidelines she gave me. Around 11:00, I started to worry that I'd get in trouble for being out too late. He argued that she didn't give me a time, and we were fine. A few minutes later, I nudged him again and said we should leave. Again, he told me to chill.

After bugging him a few more times, he yelled out in front of everyone, "DOES ANYONE HERE HAVE ANYTHING THEY DON'T FEEL LIKE WORRYING ABOUT? BECAUSE MY GIRLFRIEND WOULD LOVE TO WORRY ABOUT IT FOR YOU."

I just looked at him with hurt and disbelief. Looking back, I think that was the beginning of the end of our relationship.

We broke up two weeks before I graduated (he was a year behind me). By "broke up," I mean he unceremoniously dumped me. It threw me into a deep depression, as I was sure I would be sad and alone for the rest of my life. I think I was more terrified about my certainty that I would spend the rest of my life alone than I was upset about actually missing him. Needless to say, I survived the breakup. I went to a community college for a semester before flunking out in my second semester because of my newfound freedom. I got an apartment with friends, a full-time job, and then boomeranged back home. My worrying was always there in one form or another, but nothing memorable occurred with it until the Hit-and-Run Winter.

I don't recall the exact year it happened. I just know that over the course of a few weeks, I heard about two separate accidents in the news where a motorist hit a pedestrian and fled the scene. One report stated that authorities believed that a plow truck hit one pedestrian and may not have realized it because of the weather, road conditions, and the size of the plow on the front of the truck. I can't explain why, but this idea threw me into a tailspin.

The idea had been planted in my head that I could potentially hit and kill a pedestrian with my car and not know it. Not knowing, I could leave the scene of the accident, only to later be caught by the police and arrested. I would spend the rest of my life in prison. Writing now, I realize how ridiculous it seems, especially because I didn't drive a plow truck. I drove a 1993 Chevy Cavalier sedan. I also knew what it felt like to have my car strike something, having had the experience with another car, a road sign, and numerous snow banks.

The thing about this kind of anxiety is that it doesn't make sense. It doesn't need to make sense. If it's even the most remote possibility, it relentlessly plagues your thoughts. It attaches itself to the possibility, no matter how improbable, and hangs on for all its worth. It nags you as you're falling asleep, reminding you that it's still there, still alive, and needs to be fed. And you feed it. Because it won't stop nagging until you do. Just when you think that you've given it enough and satisfied it, it's hungry again, and the nagging starts all over again. It's almost like it has a tapeworm. You just keep feeding it, and it never reaches satiety, never puts on weight. It just gets hungrier and hungrier and requires more and more nourishment until it drives you crazy.

At that stage, I started to recognize I had an illness. I referred to it internally as simply worrying, which resulted in double checking. I was constantly worried about having killed someone. I worried about what that would do to their friends and family and about how I would survive in prison. The worry spurred the checking. Some nights, I got back in my car and retraced my route, checking to make sure that there were no signs of an accident or a victim. When I was too exhausted to do that, I'd check the local news websites, refreshing every five or ten minutes to check for any stories about a hit and run. If there was nothing on the web, I was compelled to stay up and watch the late-night news to make sure there was nothing there. Then I'd check the web some more before finally going to sleep. First thing in the morning, I was back to checking the web, the morning news, and the radio shows. On my way to work, I'd be constantly checking my rearview mirror to make sure I hadn't hit anyone. Driving in the daylight wasn't too bad, but driving in darkness was a nightmare because I knew it would make for a very long night.

I didn't know what was happening; I just knew I wanted to be free from it. I didn't want a diagnosis or coping skills. I wanted someone to make me believe there was no way I could hit a pedestrian without knowing it. I was too embarrassed to tell anyone about my thoughts, so no one knew to tell me to knock it off until I finally sought help. I had to. I could think of nothing but the imaginary pedestrians I was leaving for dead every time I got behind the wheel. It had to end.

I found a therapist who agreed to take the amount of money I could pay at the time. I explained my worrying and my checking. I told him all of it during my very first appointment with him, and I'll always remember what he said to me. He looked me straight in the eye and said, "If you hit someone, you would know it. You need to trust your senses. You're making yourself neurotic." There was probably a better way for him to put that, but it stuck. Whenever I felt myself getting sucked back into this pattern, I'd hear him saying, "You're making yourself neurotic," and it helped to set me straight. I can't say this cured me, but it helped.

I was diagnosed years later with obsessive-compulsive disorder, and although it makes sense to me now, at the time I thought that was only for people who couldn't stop washing their hands (Who knew this would be the top revolutionary medical advice to be healthy in 2020?), or had to do certain things a certain number of times, like flicking a light switch on and off five times before they can move on from it. Obsessive compulsive disorder (OCD) takes many forms, but it's not simply feeling out of sorts because your desk is disorganized. It's agonizing, it keeps you awake, it makes you sick, it's isolating, it's terrifying, and at times, it can make you wish you were dead.

I'm very fortunate I respond well to medication. I've been on and off antidepressants since I was 19, and I do much better on them. Medication helps keep my OCD symptoms in check, so anytime I feel frustrated over the side effects of the medication, I remind myself it's better than the alternative. As difficult as it can be, talking about it helps. I still feel like people look at me strangely when I share even the most surface details about my OCD, but I've learned who I can talk to and who understands. I know therapy helps. I understand going for a walk can help me sort out my thoughts. Sometimes I take good care of myself, and sometimes I eat a pint of ice cream in one sitting because the antidepressants have turned off my appetite control. I accept these things about myself and can laugh about it, but I really do sometimes wish my anxiety didn't have to make things so difficult. Difficult is not impossible. I am almost done with completing my master's degree, and I am having a sweet little baby girl in a few months. My anxiety and I will make it work; we always do.

Anxiety or no anxiety, life is beautiful.

Jenny: Growing Up in the Fast Lane

At fourteen, I was introduced to the term, *mental-health treatment.* It wasn't a polite or pleasant introduction. It started with me screaming "Fuck you!" at a police officer while throwing a stuffed animal at him. I then proceeded to tell him my life sucked, and I wished I were dead. Although I had well-developed, real-life adulting survival skills by this point, I was naïve in a lot of other ways. Blame it on the lack of the Internet back then, but I really didn't know that people actually killed themselves. It was just an expression of frustration…or so I thought.

We need to back up a little bit and set this scene properly. I'm the oldest child, and I took my role of protecting my siblings from abusive and alcoholic parents seriously. It wasn't a great situation all around. Our parents were usually drunk and often violent with each other and with us. My mother's long-time strategy when she needed a break from my dad was to call the cops and have him arrested. After they got divorced, I managed to fill a similar role in both of their lives. Dad hit me instead of Mom, and Mom yelled at me until I yelled back, and then she called the police.

At this particular time, I was working off the books at a diner. I drove Mom's car illegally to work and then to the grocery store, as someone had to work and buy food, so I did it. I was eventually able to save enough extra money to buy myself a stereo. It was the nicest thing that I had ever owned, and I loved it. For a while, it was my escape. Music helped me drown out everything around me. I could block out the bad stuff and just feel the emotions of the music. If I needed to cry or get anger out, I just picked the right song. It helped me express my emotions in a safe way. It still does.

On the night in question, I had been waiting for my mom to get home because she promised she would be home for dinner, and we could spend time together and watch "Gilmore Girls." Against my better judgment, I believed her. It got late, and she didn't come home (out drinking, I can only assume) so I went about making dinner. Dinner burned, and the kitchen filled with smoke. But I handled it. I opened the doors and aired out the house. Everything was fine. When Mom finally did get home, she was drunk, angry, and immediately began to scream and accuse me of trying to burn the house down. I stormed off to my room and turned on the stereo. After a brief screaming match about the volume, she burst into my room and cut the speaker wires.

I remember the anger. I'm sure there were other emotions hidden there as well. She had no right to destroy something I had worked so hard to get for myself. I shouldn't have even been working in the first place. I lost it. I started yelling back. And…the police were called. It was a familiar pattern. I also remember just being so tired and so done with all of it. So, even after I had calmed down a bit and stopped throwing my furry weapons, when the officer asked what was going on, I simply told him that life sucked and I wished I was dead.

In what seemed like seconds later, I was handcuffed and in the back of his police car. I had no idea what the hell was going on now. This did not fit the pattern at all. Was I being arrested for throwing a stuffed animal at him? For swearing? I saw the back of a police car once before, as my dad had asked me to bring him his shoes one time as the police were pulling him outside, but I had never been inside one.

I tried to calm myself down. Nothing was working. I was terrified, and I had no idea what to do next. So finally, as a last-ditch effort, I told myself this wasn't real. It was just a scene in a movie or something. I imagined I was a really badass criminal and began my debut performance—taunting the officer and acting like I didn't have a care in the world. This actually managed to calm me down a little bit as I got lost in the part. It did not improve the situation. The officer was clearly annoyed and told me that I had two choices. I could go to the hospital or juvenile detention. I looked at my mother, still drunk and in the passenger seat of the police car and made my decision. I wasn't sick. I wasn't stupid. To the hospital we go.

When we got to the emergency room, I was told I was going to be evaluated, whatever that meant. They took my blood pressure and weight. Listened to my lungs. Normal doctor things. And then they left me waiting in the exam room. After a few hours, a nurse came to check on me, and I asked her if I could go home. She told me that they were waiting for a bed to admit me to the adult psychiatric unit.

Huh? I had no idea what that meant. I knew "psycho" meant "crazy," but that was about the extent of my understanding. Before I could figure it out, I was in a locked unit with some interesting adults. It turns out that the "loony bin" isn't just a random thing that people say. It's an actual place. To this day, I remember a lot of things about the hospitalization and the people I met there. Throughout my first days there, I studied them all, like they were characters in my movie. I was trying to figure out the plot.

One of the nurses there was the first person I remember being kind to me in a long time. I remember thinking I wished my mom could be more like her. After about a week, I was released to a group home; I was told with the intention of giving me a more stable home environment. That lasted about a week before another kid living there threatened me with a kitchen knife. One of us had to be moved. She didn't have anywhere else to go and I did, so I was sent back home.

Things didn't exactly calm down. Over the next few years, this became the new pattern. We'd fight, Mom would call the police, and I would get taken away to the hospital or to residential treatment centers. Some were better experiences than others. The hospital had given me shots to calm me down, which scared me a lot. Eventually though, I ended up at a residential treatment center for several months.

Once I got there, I had a consistent therapist who listened to me. The staff were all actually trying to take care of me, and I became attached to them. They gave me a place to stay, three meals a day, and no one hurt me. I was safe.

Not to say it was entirely smooth sailing. At some point early on, I was really upset and crying hysterically. I felt like everything inside of me was being released somehow. I didn't want to wake up my roommate, so I went out into the hall, which was against the rules. The night staff, whom I didn't know very well, tried to get me to go back to bed. I wouldn't go, and I wasn't able to explain what was happening. They didn't understand. I got more and more upset and ultimately ended up spending a few hours in a padded room-type situation (another thing that I didn't know existed outside of the movies).

The staff's diagnosis about what was going on with me shifted over time. At first, they said I was bipolar. Then it was borderline personality disorder. They tried a bunch of medications that didn't really help. Finally, we figured out that the real problem was severe anxiety. I didn't know anxiety could come out in a lot of different ways, including as anger. As they explained to me, anger is a strong emotion that helps you flee from danger and protect yourself, even if you're afraid. It was a survival instinct. In the end, they said I needed three things: coping strategies, a stable home, and parental authority. I was the grown-up in my own house, and that wasn't going to change. Now, the coping strategies thing we were able to work on.

I learned to control the anger, in a lot of ways, because I understood it was triggered by intense anxiety. When I felt the anxiety starting, I could do things to try to control it before it reached the point of the explosive anger. This understanding helped me in both staying out of further legal trouble and being able to manage my ongoing anxiety problems going forward. I still struggle with my anxiety, although not as much with anger anymore. I judge myself constantly and worry other people are always judging me, too. I'm constantly trying to make sure people like and approve of me. I never want to let anyone down. I feel the most insecure around people whom I believe are smarter than me, especially those with a college education. I fear being seen as uneducated, so I compensate by speaking so quickly that I run my words together and end up presenting poorly. I feel judged and automatically think I am inferior. I don't know why; it is just a fear I have. I ask myself, *why can't I just play the part of someone whom I admire and think is intelligent, and pretend I have an advanced degree? I have learned so much in life, and I am a smart, capable person.*

Why do I struggle to believe this? I know in my heart it is true, but I am still working on convincing my brain.

Most of the time, this is a low-level concern. It doesn't stop me from going about my day and living my life. Sometimes, I feed a fleeting thought until it grows into a monster. Then the real panic sets in. When the anxiety wins, I can't breathe. It feels like someone has put their fist down my throat. I can't breathe in or out. My heart starts to flutter really fast, my thoughts race, and my hands shake. Then I worry people will see my hands shaking and think I am an alcoholic. I am not. But why wouldn't they think I am since my parents are? It's not a fun spiral. I'm continuing to learn ways to manage it all of the time.

Today, my mom is in recovery, we are a part of each other's lives, and my dad is in my life. I know they love me, despite their struggles. I'm married to a wonderful and loving man and pursuing an acting career. I aspire to become a famous actress and have a platform to advocate and talk about anxiety and use my life experiences to help others.

I hope one day we meet again when you see me on the big screen.

Jackie: The Lion Tamer

I feel obligated to share two things off the bat: I am not a licensed mental-health professional. I am certainly not a substitute for one. Any advice I give is based less on cutting-edge research than what has worked for me and for the people I know. I'm hoping it will help you or your loved one, too. Also, anxiety is not the same for everyone. These are my personal experiences.

Well then, let's get to know each other a little bit. I'm a woman in my mid-twenties and currently in school to become a physician assistant. I have been officially diagnosed with attention deficit disorder and polycystic ovarian syndrome; however, I'm otherwise healthy and dare I say, *typical*. My anxiety issues are undiagnosed, but not untreated. If I were to categorize myself, I'd call it "functional social anxiety with a dash of general anxiety."

Both of my parents are from families where mental-health issues are considered shameful. They are to be handled discretely, if at all. On top of that, when I was first considering seeing a provider, I had concerns about my insurance company knowing or a diagnosis affecting my future rates. I was also worried about whether it would affect my ability to receive scholarships or work for the military (not that I ended up taking this path).

As such, until I was 21, I kept my struggle pretty private and utilized the Internet, my friends, my mother, and myself to help me cope and function. At the end of my junior year of college, I decided to utilize the free counselors and ended up receiving both individual and group therapy.

I know most people have, at one time, experienced some form of anxiety. It's a natural emotion meant to keep people motivated or cautious. My therapist in college sent me an article about an experiment involving fish. Some of the fish were naturally cautious, and some were naturally bold. Which fish flourished was dependent on the environment. My therapist's point was that both were natural variations, and neither was "better" than the other. I went to therapy trying to completely rid myself of anxiety, but the goal ended up being to keep the feelings and struggles manageable.

Our brain is designed to experience anxiety in short bursts, not the prolonged foamy lathers of duress that my (and maybe your) neuroses seem to enjoy. My personal preferred metaphor is that the prolonged anxiety feels as though a lion were on the verge of devouring you all the time. The game is convincing yourself the lion is not in the room. When it is, I assure you, you will know it. Some people require medication to recognize the lion is not in the room and act accordingly, even as their mind is telling them otherwise.

For me, anxiety is feeling tight-chested and uneasy. I can't relax. It feels like checking your grade when you think you failed a test. It feels like walking into a room of people you want to like you but you suspect don't. It feels like a first date or an important job interview. It feels like sitting in the waiting room waiting to see if a loved one survived risky surgery. I obsess over whatever is causing me anxiety. It's difficult, if not impossible, to take my mind off of it (after all, what do you think about when I tell you not to think about pink elephants? If you answered anything other than pink elephants, color me impressed). Nonetheless, I try to retain a logical thought process.

From the beginning, I know it is anxiety working to take over my thoughts. There is no good reason for it. Most of the time, I can talk myself through it. The feelings of anxiety, tension, and uneasiness remain, but I use logic and willpower to push myself to do what I need to in order to function. I feel like a lion is in the room, but I act as though it's not.

The problem is, even though I can often control it to a degree, this doesn't come easily or automatically. The effort it takes to overpower my anxiety is the equivalent of making myself keep running on a treadmill, speak publicly, clean the apartment, etc. I can do those things, but they each require a certain amount of energy. If I'm already drained, I can't push myself into doing it or I end up doing it halfway. Some might argue that it's a lack of self-discipline and drive. Maybe to some extent it is since we all have varying amounts of both. However, that is certainly not the only factor. Pushing through anxiety is like pushing yourself to run a long distance. Some people are naturally better at it. The more you do it, the better you get at it. Even if you have the ability, if you don't have the motivation and drive to work at it, you will have difficulty getting there. Some people need medications and training to get there. For me, the cornerstones for coping with my anxiety are: research, therapy, medication, and drive.

Research. Know the beast to conquer it. This was my first step. The Internet contains a ridiculous amount of useful resources. I noticed that situations involving human interaction, whether it was going to a party or going to the grocery store, were what tended to give me the most anxiety. Sometimes I would literally wake up anxious for no reason, but more often than not, it was the "social" situations that caused the problem. So, I started researching social anxiety and what the common symptoms and common treatments were. Knowledge is power. Arm yourself with it.

Therapy. My research informed me that social anxiety was best treated with therapy (particularly group therapy and/or cognitive behavioral therapy). So, instead of seeking out a psychiatrist, I decided a psychologist at my school was a solid first stop. Therapy was extremely helpful for me. Since the school was paying my doctor, I didn't feel like a burden talking to him about my problems. Guilt is something I frequently struggle with, so eliminating that was helpful for me. It was also useful to talk to someone with knowledge and insight into my issues who was unbiased and eager to help. It allowed me to unpack and organize my thoughts and get knowledgeable feedback.

On one occasion, I started talking about something I thought only vaguely bothered me and then started crying. And I like to think I know myself pretty well! I find it uncomfortable to talk about the things that hurt me or wear me down, and therapy wasn't an exception. The discomfort was worth the insight though.

Note, I feel that it needs to be said that you get what you put into therapy. You have to want therapy to work. You also have to be honest. I can turn on the charm and lie and convince a new therapist that I'm a "normal" person without any anxiety. I convince the world on a regular basis. Sometimes it's not even a lie. But what's the point in doing that with therapists? Why bother seeing them in the first place? Be honest with them so they can help you. Also, you must be ready to at least consider the idea that your therapist has insights you don't. If you are not open, then any time he or she says something you disagree with or don't want to hear, you will disregard it, allowing yourself to live in denial. How will you ever get better like that?

The key to this step is trusting your provider. Now, I'm not saying just trust any therapist you happen to meet. Do research on them to know they are competent. Check their reputations and credentials. If you start seeing one provider, and you're not feeling comfortable or you don't trust him or her, try another. There's no shame in searching around to find a good fit. That being said, if you've gone through ten psychologists, and you still can't find someone you trust, then you probably need to do a little self-reflection on what the real problem is here. I'm certainly not suggesting finding a person who will only tell you things you want to hear.

Support. Do you have friends or family you trust? Utilize them. I found this to be extremely difficult for a number of reasons. I was ashamed. I didn't want to burden anyone. I was functioning halfway decently, so was anything really wrong with me? So, what if it was hard? Maybe I was just a whiner. Eventually I worked up to opening up to one friend. It was hard, but I learned to talk about it. Now, I've told multiple people about my anxiety issues, and I have a number of people I can talk to when it gets bad. This is invaluable to me. I always found writing about what was bothering me helped me stop building it up in my head. Talking it out helps me. Letting the crazy, obsessive worries out in a coherent manner gives them less power over me and makes me feel a lot better. It doesn't go away but feels more manageable. Friends and family can often calm and reassure me. They often tell me what I already know, but it's reassuring to hear it. Love and support can't cure my anxiety, but it does help ease the burden.

Drive. Just as you have to want therapy to work in order to reap benefits, you have to want to overcome your anxiety issues and achieve a better quality of life for yourself. And you have to be willing to work for it. This is perhaps the hardest part of trying to overcome anxiety, because anxiety itself is already so mentally and physically draining, which is why I would suggest enlisting people to help you. Utilize whoever is appropriate (be it your family, your therapist, your significant other, your friends) to hold you accountable, help you stay organized, help you make appointments, do other chores for you so you're less drained, etc.

Accountability is important. The easy thing, the thing that gives me the most immediate relief (if any relief is possible that day), is to give in to the compulsions and to avoid whatever situation is causing the anxiety in the first place. This is a tool to be used. Use it as a crutch. Some days, I'm exhausted. The very thought of leaving my apartment to go to the grocery store is draining. Some days, I don't go. That's completely fine, because most days, I do go. If I stop going to the grocery store (and get someone to do it for me or enlist in an online delivery service so I don't have to go), that's when we have a problem. When you become dependent on giving in to your anxiety to get through it, that's a problem.

It's important to recognize when your anxiety gets the best of you, and you need your crutch. For most people, anxiety is a chronic issue. There are going to be bad days. It's not a reflection on your character. But also recognize when you're able to overcome it and do what you want to or have to do. Celebrate successes and forgive lapses. Analyze why you do or don't use your crutch in certain situations. Therapy can be very helpful with this, with helping you recognize the patterns within yourself. What makes some days worse or better? What situations are worse or better? Why?

Be open and honest with yourself and others. Reach out and connect with whoever gets you and helps you cope. Believe in yourself and know you have options and resources. Find your people. They are out there. Life is good.

Part III

JOURNEYS TO UNDERSTANDING:
THE KIDS ARE ALL RIGHT

Primer on Anxiety in Children

In parallel to our earlier discussion about the differences between *normal anxiety* and *pathologic anxiety* (or as we prefer to think about it, anxiety vs. ANXIETY), similar concepts apply to children. All children experience anxiety in their daily lives and as a normal part of development. Where to draw the line between normal and pathologic anxiety is difficult, especially since kids don't often have the language or reasoning to explain in depth (or at least in adult language) what is going on inside their minds. Complicating that, kids are continually growing, developing, and changing. Having new (and even fairly severe) anxieties seemingly overnight could be either the first symptoms of an anxiety disorder or a sign of normal development. At baseline, kids have very poor insight into their anxiety or how to deal with it. They are forced to rely on the adults in their lives to interpret their outward behavior as a sign of how they are doing mentally.

And it's tricky. Sometimes our tendency as parents or even as healthcare providers is to minimize anxieties or chalk them up to "normal kid stuff." Most of the time, this is true. Most fears throughout childhood are developmentally appropriate, but about 23% represent true anxiety disorders.[2] The clearest example of a developmentally appropriate fear that most parents will relate to is stranger danger. Babies, prior to six months of age, don't generally really mind being passed around between adults. Generally, around 7-10 months of age, they suddenly develop a fear of people they don't know. This can be intense. It can last until two years of age and still be considered normal. But as you've gotten used to me saying by now, it's all a matter of degrees. If it continues into preschool-aged years or reaches the point where normal activities like playing with friends or going to school are becoming a problem, they may need help with taming the fear.

There is research into normative fears of childhood. This is a kind of map of "normal" fears by age and in many ways, they make sense. What's important to keep in mind is kids can have very intense fears that, even if the fear itself is normal for their age, still crosses the line into an anxiety disorder. In fact, most anxiety disorders in kids are seen for the first time in childhood, and the exact anxiety disorders we see vary by age and are generally more extreme versions of the same kinds of normal fears we would expect for this age group. Basically, the relationship between *normal anxiety* and *pathologic anxiety* can be even more complicated in kids.

Here is a very brief introduction:

Infancy and Young Toddlers
Infants are generally overly fearful of immediate, concrete threats in their environment.[4] It's rare for infants and toddlers to be overly concerned with what is going to happen in the future—their brains just don't work this way. The types of common fears are things like strangers or being separated from caregivers. Going along with their in-the-moment style of thinking, these things are generally only truly upsetting to them in the moment. It's rare, although not necessarily a sign of a problem, for kids this young to be afraid of things that may happen in the future. Although concerning patterns of behavior that

warrant further monitoring can be noted at this age, anxiety disorders are not typically diagnosed. Signs of more intense fear and anxiety can include things like sleep disturbances and defiant behavior.

Older Toddlers and Young Childhood

Children (starting as young as age 3) begin to show fear of things that might happen and focus more on imaginary or abstract fears rather than things that are currently happening. This is often seen with the development of fears of things like the dark, fires, water, or thunder and lightning.[4] These more abstract things have likely never caused the child any harm, but at this age, they are first able to comprehend that they could potentially be harmful and begin to show fear towards them. Slightly later in childhood, this can extend to fears of things like death or others dying (usually around preschool age). This is thought to be a similar situation in which the fear develops around this age because it is the first-time children develop the cognitive ability to recognize the threat.

Signs of distress at this age can include crying, clinging, social withdrawal, avoidance of certain people or objects they find threatening, and bedwetting (after being fully toilet trained). Although the fears themselves are age appropriate, at the extremes, they can be diagnosed as disorders at this age including separation anxiety disorders, specific phobias, panic disorders, or even early forms of generalized anxiety disorder. The good news is these disorders often respond well to treatment; usually this involves some sort of child-centered therapy. In older children (about ages 8-13), this often involves both the parents and the child. For children younger than that, parents may meet with a therapist alone for guidance and training on how best to help their child's anxiety without the child seeing a therapist often (or at all).[2]

School Age/Adolescence

By this point, many of the common anxieties of childhood tend to more closely represent those that we would see in adults, with some increased focus on peer groups relative to adults. Common fears include school performance, natural disasters, illness, and peer rejection.[4] Similarly, signs of distress start to more closely resemble those of adults: withdrawal, extreme shyness, inner feelings of shame and distress. So does treatment. Although kids may need some extra help in learning how to express and tame their emotions, many of the same general strategies of therapies or medications that are used with adults can be used in this age group with good results.

It's a Girl!

In January 1993, my life forever changed when I gave birth to a beautiful, healthy baby girl. She has brought me unimaginable joy.

From the moment I became a mother, my sole purpose became clear: To do everything in my power to ensure she was unconditionally loved, happy, healthy, successful, and surrounded by family and friends while living the life she chose and making the world a better place. No big deal, right? *Wrong.* It is actually quite a big deal.

I discovered, to my great dismay, that I can't fix everything. I told my kids they could tell me anything. I would not judge them. It was important for them to know they could never do anything to push me away. And so they told me the good and bad. To be honest, some of it I wish I didn't know. Our openness built the strong relationship we have today. No subject, opinion, or problem is off limits. We even talk politics on occasion!

As I reflect on raising my children, I am reminded of the challenges we tackled together as a family. I think about what I could have done differently, better. Should my husband and I have gotten divorced sooner? Would that have resulted in less stress and anxiety for our children? For us? What if I had found more effective treatment for, in retrospect, the clear signs of anxiety within our family? I can't change the past, but that doesn't prevent me from thinking about it and wishing I could.

During my 29 years of marriage, we experienced many challenges together. Some brought us closer, and others created unresolvable conflict and anger. In 1997, my husband was driving to work in the early morning when his vehicle was hit head on by a drunk driver. The drunk driver and his passenger both died at the scene. It was a serious and life-changing event, not only for my husband, but also, for our entire family.

This traumatic experience impacted Nicole deeply. At four years old, she began to think about the possibility of losing her father and then other people she loved. It triggered worries about death and her health and safety.

Nicole is intelligent, beautiful, and compassionate. She was born inquisitive and has always been a bit intense. When she was seven, we had her IQ tested and she scored in the top percentile for her age group with exceptional abilities to read, reason, and solve mathematical and analytical problems. I made assumptions associating her continuous and unanswerable (at least by me) questions to her advanced ability to understand and process information. The reality was her concerns were missed signs of anxiety.

I recall during elementary school, sitting on Nicole's bed night after night rubbing her back and reassuring her as she tried to sleep. She was worried about so many things; honestly, it seemed like everything. She feared never waking up. She didn't trust her brain would keep her heart beating while she slept. She wanted to know how her brain functioned and why she should trust it to wake her up. She was afraid of dying in her sleep. Tough questions from a first grader.

So, I slept with her and monitored her breathing. I reassured her she would be fine. I hugged her and made promises to keep her safe, all while wondering why she was always afraid and how I could make the fear go away. Why was I unable to make my child feel safe? Was something medically wrong with her? Was I doing this parenting thing wrong?

When 9/11 happened, it shook the entire world. We live an hour outside of New York City. This act of terrorism hit close to home and affected people we knew. That day and those attacks had a compounding impact on Nicole's sense of how safe, or rather, unsafe, she is in an uncertain and scary world.

Around that time, Nicole wrote a poem with a black and white picture of a tree in winter with no leaves. I was struck by how sad it was. I didn't know how to help her feel safer and less alone. It never occurred to me that she could be depressed at such a young age. Sad maybe, but not depressed. That was for adults. Right?

She wrote:

> *I am a branch*
> *All alone*
> *It is so cold*
> *All my beautiful and colorful leaves,*
> *Are gone*
> *Twigs around me*
> *Are Falling*
> *Down to the hard ground*
> *What if my twigs are next?*
> *Then I will really be alone*
> *I feel weak,*
> *On this cold winter day.*

As Nicole entered adolescence, she felt her throat closing and couldn't breathe. This was terrifying for all of us, especially her. Allergies, we assumed. We rushed her to the emergency room many times. Each time her oxygen rate was fine. They referred us to specialists to determine if she had sinus or tonsil issues. She did not.

We left every doctors appointment without a diagnosis. Nicole started to see a therapist. I needed to stop her suffering. It became clear these repeated events were terrifying but not life threatening. It is my hope mental-health treatment has advanced over the past twenty years and today, we would be referred to a psychiatrist.

As Nicole entered junior high school, she was exhausted. Her body ached, and her stomach and head hurt. She spent most days in bed. She was moody, grumpy, and sad. She didn't feel well and couldn't go to school. She just wanted to sleep. We took her to doctor after doctor. All we wanted was a diagnosis. If we had one, it would allow us to treat her, to do something to make it better.

One of those countless specialists eventually diagnosed her with fibromyalgia. I was relieved—there was a reason she felt like this. *Wrong again.* Turns out all they gave us was false hope. They were the professionals, the ones we were counting on for answers. I still wonder if they understood how desperately we needed a real solution.

Not one of the doctors mentioned depression or anxiety. Did they miss that rotation in medical school? They told us to keep her active and insist she get up and go to school. They actually medically prescribed having her *be more active* as their advice. Really. I went to them because I couldn't get her out of bed. So they told me to get her out of bed. Brilliant. Were they listening at all? I would go into her room each morning and attempt to wake her up. She would cry or yell at me and say she didn't feel well. She would not get up. She was truly miserable and in pain.

As this developed into a pattern, I became overwhelmed by my inability to get her to go to school. I worried she would fall behind in her classes and lose contact with her friends—basically, disappear from her own life. My husband expected me to get her out of bed and to follow the doctor's advice. "Just make her. Be the parent." I couldn't make her; she wasn't up to it. It didn't seem like forcing her was going to solve anything. The tension in our house continued to build. I didn't want to do it anymore. How could I make her life any harder and cause her more pain? Yet, I kept trying.

Night after night, I lay awake freaking out about getting her up in the morning, fearing the conflict that would descend on our family when I again failed. What kind of mother couldn't get her child to school? Everything got worse. The hurt, disappointment, and anger continued. I remember each night just praying, *please give her the strength to get up and go to school.*

One morning, Nicole looked at me through tears after my third attempt and accused me of caring more about getting her to go to school than about her. I saw the pain in her eyes. That was it for me. Regardless of the consequences, I wasn't going to force her to get up. My efforts were only making her feel like a failure. More stress and guilt wasn't the answer.

I pressured her less. She eventually began to occasionally go in late. Slowly, she gained more control and went to school a few days a week. I promised her I would leave work and pick her up at any time without questions. And I did.

A panic attack is an emotional and physical attack on your body and mind. They are difficult to describe, heartbreaking to watch, and painful to endure. Nicole broke her ankle. A few weeks after it was casted, I went into her bedroom, and she was crying hysterically, telling me she couldn't breathe. She told me she had further injured her ankle, that it was swelling, and the cast was cutting off her circulation. She needed it off, right now.

Although her panic was very real, it made no sense to me. Yet there she was yelling, "Get it off!" I didn't know what to do, so I called the on-call pediatrician. The doctor had literally no idea what I wanted or needed. Understandable, since I didn't either. I tried to reassure Nicole how unlikely it was that she had further broken her ankle. She couldn't hear me.

I failed at calming her down. So, I agreed in a rainstorm late at night, to take her to the emergency room. As we were driving to the hospital, she became quiet. I pulled over and she whispered, "Mom, we can go home now."

Seriously? What the hell? Now it didn't hurt after we ventured out in the middle of the night in a storm. So, home we went. She was exhausted and went to bed. I tucked her in, kissed her goodnight, and spent the night thinking, *what the hell just happened?*

Nicole was depressed, lacked self-confidence, and needed to be part of something positive outside of our family and the stress in our house. She desperately wanted to fit in somewhere. I believe now that she also needed medication. Over time, she found the strength to re-engage in her life. She needed a reason to get out of bed. She was shy and searching for acceptance and understanding. She wanted friends, to be accepted, and to fit into the brutal world of high school (you know "Mean Girls"—they truly exist).

Around this time, a friend of my father's referred Nicole for a job at a local restaurant. She started at fourteen and worked there for over six years. She loved that job. It changed her life. She fit in and began to feel accepted and capable. Her self-confidence increased. She made friends. She enjoyed being a part of something. She was constantly busy. She excelled and flourished. Her symptoms decreased. She went to school…most days. She worked thirty hours a week. She became the yearbook editor.

Nicole graduated as the Salutatorian of her high school. She gave a speech at graduation about change and how when she and her peers started high school, nothing was more important than not being different and fitting in. But now, as they leave high school, actually nothing is more important than being yourself, growing as an individual, facing the fear of the unknown, and the freedom to be ready and open for new and unfamiliar experiences. She ended her speech with words of encouragement centered on the idea that in high school you could succeed by just getting by, but now, in the real world, graduates needed to become the best at whatever they truly loved and pursue it with focus and passion for the rest of their lives.

She reassured her classmates they were prepared and ready. And it turned out so was she.

I always told Nicole she could do anything she set her mind to…you know, the mom speech. So, of course, this advice she took to heart. Nicole decided to go away to college. By "away," I mean 20 hours from home. She is one of the bravest people I know. She had significant issues with being homesick her entire childhood. She needed to be home and close to us…to be kept safe. Now, she knew by avoiding doing things that make her anxious, she would reinforce her fears. She wanted to prove to herself she could go away to college and not, out of fear, make the safe choice. Off to college she went.

During a Thanksgiving break from college, we went to the grocery store to get snacks to eat while binge watching on Netflix. We were both looking forward to our evening together. In the middle of picking out popcorn, Nicole suddenly turned to me and urged, "We have to leave, now."

Confused, I left the shopping cart in the aisle and ran after her. When we got to the car, she was crying uncontrollably and insisting something terrible was about to happen, and she needed to get home immediately. I thought, *okay, this is an easy one, we are only a few miles from home.*

Then it hit me—she wasn't talking about her childhood home less than a mile away. She was talking about her home in Chicago. Logically, it was the night before Thanksgiving, and her entire family was coming the next day. Flying home immediately was not at all feasible, and there were probably no flights. But that isn't what she needed to hear. On some level, she already knew. What she needed wasn't logic; she needed to regain control. I wanted Nicole to know whatever she did next was her choice, and I supported it. I didn't want her to be stressed by worrying that what she needed to do wasn't going to be okay. Validating her feelings and giving her time to work through it was as important as not making her feel it was ridiculous, and that she had to explain what she was feeling.

We sat in the parking lot for a long time. Nicole frantically looked up flights on her cell phone through her tears. I told her if she could find a flight, I would take her to the airport. Although she didn't understand and couldn't explain her fear, it was overwhelming. On top of this stress, she worried her family would be mad if she left and would think she was weird. How could they understand? We agreed to go back to my house and continue looking for flights. When we got back, we retreated to her childhood bedroom as she paced and tried to calm down. She took some medicine and began to breathe a little better. She laid down and fell asleep.

Although panic attacks are not actually physically harmful, they can make you feel like and think you are truly dying. It is important to remember the symptoms are a normal response of your body fighting danger. The difference is the threat is coming from inside your body as opposed to an external threat, and often, there seems to be no reason. The symptoms are real and terrifying. They include: trouble breathing (feeling like you are being smothered), racing heart, chest pain, hot flashes, feeling like you are choking, being dizzy, nauseous, numbness, being afraid you are dying, losing control, or going insane.

We made it through the night. The next day, Nicole was exhausted but all right. It would have only added to her stress to invalidate her feelings. It would have been hurtful to tell her she was being unreasonable or to agree her family would not understand. She already knew. Logic was the last thing she needed. Nicole needed to know I was there, and that I didn't think she was crazy.

Then one year during midterms, the call came. You know the call. Every parent knows the call—the one you spend your life fearing—the one that stops your world and takes your breath away. Your child is in danger. Real danger! I can't adequately express the terror.

I was at a memorial service for my grandmother, Nana, when Nicole called. I went outside to answer the phone, and *all* I heard was her crying, gasping for air, and saying she couldn't do it anymore. Couldn't do *what* anymore? I panicked. I mean, really panicked. Did she mean she was going to hurt herself? She said she was depressed and overwhelmed. She had not been able to get out of bed for days. I was on the next flight.

I arrived the following day sleepless, exhausted, and petrified. I went straight to the bed and breakfast across the street from the college where I always stay. She was sitting on the steps in the rain when my cab pulled up. I jumped out and hugged her as if both of our lives depended on how much I could love her. She was shaking and crying. I was certain by being there I could help her get back into balance. I could fix everything. For the first time in her life, I could-n't. That hit us both hard.

Nothing worked. She wasn't sleeping and kept obsessing about how she was going to fail and ruin her entire future. Catastrophic thinking took over. She believed this moment in time would result in a failure so profound, that literally her entire life was over. The anxiety had taken control. She could not see there were choices and options. I was confident she could get back on track even if she failed midterms or took a semester off, but in that moment, she was unable to see this as an option. As Nicole was sitting on the bed in our room freaking out about a paper she needed to write, she began to scratch her arms and act erratically. I became truly petrified and knew we needed help. I had never seen her act like that before and was truly frightened.

I called around frantically. I could not find anywhere to take her for mental-health treatment. I felt so confused and useless. I tried the college counseling office, then did a Google search, and found one mental-health inpatient facility. I called, and they were at capacity. Looking back, I am so very grateful. Years later, I learned that avoiding hospitalization of youth at the onset of a first episode can help prevent a negative self-image and help prevent them from defining themselves by their mental-health diagnosis. Feel free to read that last sentence a second time. It is one of the most powerful points I make.

I called my friend, Robyn. I was close to hysterical and desperate. It felt like my child was drowning, and I couldn't swim. I couldn't save her. Robyn is an experienced, licensed mental-health professional. She told me we simply needed to get Nicole immediate medical treatment. We could figure the rest out later. I called a taxi, and we headed to the emergency room.

As we arrived at the hospital, I was outwardly calm, but truly terrified. The fear for my child was at a level I had never experienced. The noise of the emergency room and the people and lights fused together. I felt like I was watching a movie of a tragedy or horror film. I was numb and trying to stay focused. What was going on? How were we going to fix this? I didn't even understand what *this* was. The nurse led us to an exam room, and a young, personable neurologist came in and introduced himself. He was kind and calm. He treated her like a regular patient. He asked her about her symptoms and what she was studying in college. It was all strangely normal. Meanwhile, I was convincing myself our world as we knew it had ended. But he had a different view. He said she needed to rest and reset. They gave her two shots and she slept and slept and slept. I started crying as I stepped outside and called Robyn again.

I was unsure of everything. Would Nicole recover? Was she having a breakdown? Was she mentally ill? Would she be able to stay in college? What did this mean for her future? Would this prevent her from achieving her goals and dreams? Was this temporary? What additional ongoing medical treatment would she need? Would she be safe? Should she leave college and come home? If she did, then what?

Once she woke up, the doctor asked how she was feeling, and they talked more about her life. I didn't realize it, but in that moment, in these discussions, he was reinforcing that she still had a life…one she could still live. She could go back to college and achieve her goals. He talked about ways she needed to learn to manage her symptoms and explained it was not unusual for these issues to surface during college. He recommended she follow up with a psychiatrist, gave her a prescription, and told her to find a therapist.

I will be forever grateful for this young, insightful doctor. He was progressive in his views about mental health. He treated her symptoms, helped her, gave us information on her medical condition, and reassured us both she could manage it—just like you would with diabetes. His gift to us was so simple and yet so profound. He treated her as a patient with physical symptoms (she needed rest, to get some sleep, and a reset). He helped us understand her medical symptoms could be treated. One of the hardest things I ever did was leave her at college and go home. We sat on her bed in her dorm room, and she asked me what she should do. We were both crying, and I honestly didn't know. The stakes were high. They were her life! Finally she looked at me and said, "I am staying, but you must leave now before I change my mind." She was in pain and clearly not okay. I was at a crossroads and didn't know what to do. All of me wanted her to come home where I could be sure she was safe. I didn't tell her that. If she stayed and hurt herself, I wouldn't be able to live with myself. I can still see her lying on her pink- and white-flowered comforter on her tiny dorm room bed with tears streaming down her face as I hugged her and got up and walked out of her room. I did not want her to think I doubted her ability to go on and succeed, but I did. I really did. I was terrified. It felt like a true life or death decision.

Today, Nicole still has days when she is exhausted from the effort it takes to fight her anxiety and live life, but she handles it. A couple of years ago, Nicole called me and said, "I am fine, but…" Not a good sign. She told me she had been coping with her anxiety by isolating herself to reserve her energy, which had manifested to the point where she had been unable to physically leave her bedroom to even go to the kitchen. She had been in her room for two days. I remained calm and asked her what her plan was. She said her room-mate had been bringing her what she needed and had agreed he and his girlfriend would go to her place to give Nicole some space. She called her doctor who called in a new prescription.

Over the next few days, Nicole emerged and found the coping skills to get out of her room and back to her life. I am confident each time her anxiety battles for control, Nicole will win.

It's a Boy!

In December of 1994, I got the best Christmas present ever when I gave birth to a robust, adorable, little boy. James stole my heart and brings laughter and love into my world every day.

I knew my daughter had anxiety issues. What I completely missed, as I was focused on her, was that my son was also struggling with anxiety.

He was painfully shy from an early age. Although he was extremely shy, he seemed to enjoy activities like Boy Scouts and sports with his friends. In kindergarten, he met a group of boys, and they all became good friends. The boys all grew up together, and my husband and I were friends with their parents. They were always together whether in school, on weekends, at camp, or on vacation. James felt he belonged. He was comfortable, or so I believed. To my knowledge, he didn't have thoughts of inadequacy and constantly being judged. Boy, was I wrong.

It never occurred to me James had anxiety or that he was being bullied. He didn't have pressure to make friends growing up. He had plenty. In high school when he still refused to talk on the phone or go into a store alone, I still thought he was just shy. It was his personality. We didn't know he had severe social anxiety.

Why would we think a kid with an active social life had anxiety, especially social anxiety? I have learned social anxiety isn't about not wanting to be around people; it is fearing what people you are around think about you. I didn't understand all the ways anxiety presents itself. When James was three, he started having pain in his knees and experiencing stomach issues. We took him to a specialist in Westchester who said he had a rheumatic issue. He was growing so fast, it was causing pain. To this day, we have not been able to solve all of James's intestinal issues. I focused on him from a purely medical perspective. That was a mistake.

In high school and college, if he was running even a few seconds late to a class, James would not enter the classroom; he felt everyone would stare at him and judge him. He gets concerned about being the center of attention. He worries constantly that whatever he is doing, he won't do it well enough.

When James has multiple things to get done, he is overwhelmed. I mean completely panicked. When he has a research or term paper due, he works on it daily even if it isn't due for a month. He will create a plan for what to do each day to reassure himself he can get it done on time. The constant pressure to get it done weighs on him and creates stress until the assignment is completed.

At fourteen, James started working as a busboy at the same restaurant as his sister. Although working there was a blessing for her, it was torture for him. Each time he had to approach a table, he became anxious, and when customers were rude to him, he would hide in the kitchen. I didn't know he was being bullied by his fears and anxiety.

James hates to read. In high school, when he went to a learning center for help with SAT prep, we learned he had a learning disability that affects his rate of comprehension. My mother and I have dyslexia, and although it isn't the same, it is a related condition. He spends hours reading and taking notes to understand the material before he can study. This requires a substantial investment of time before each test. He put in the extra effort and graduated from college with honors with a B.A. in Athletic Training.

Now that James knows he has anxiety, he is working to understand and manage it. A few years ago, he secured a position as a graduate assistant and began pursuing his master's degree in Kinesiology with a concentration in Exercise Physiology. In this role, he taught lab classes. This, as you can imagine, was a monumental challenge. James was determined to overcome his fears. And he did.

He taught for a semester and then moved down south. He took jobs as a personal trainer, a stretch therapist, a peace officer for the town, and a bouncer at a local bar. A few months ago, he was accepted into the Feinberg School of Medicine at Northwestern and has the opportunity to go pursue getting his Doctor of Physical Therapy degree. He is also considering a different path: pursuing becoming a Licensed Clinical Social Worker. He has proven he has the courage and drive to succeed at whatever he chooses. I hope he sees it, too! I am proud of the man he is today.

I missed many of the signs and symptoms in my children, especially my son, as they were growing up. I didn't understand depression, mood swings, unpredictable bouts of anger or irritability, lack of self-confidence, sensitivity to change, and obsessive behavior could all be related to anxiety. The good news is, the kids turned out great.

I have learned so much. I hope they feel my unconditional love for them. Not being judgmental and ensuring they know they can never do anything to push me away is important.

My son wrote me a note when he was in college that said: "Thanks for always putting family first and helping me become the man I am…thanks for being there for me when I screw up and helping me find solutions or just find the good that's still there…thanks for being the one person I can get all my anger out on and knowing that I don't mean anything I say during the moments when I'm stressed. I definitely wouldn't be as compassionate as I am if you hadn't shown me as much compassion as you have throughout my whole life."

Sometimes just letting someone know you are in their corner is enough. It is also all you can really do.

Parenting is hard. It is all consuming. You have no idea what you are doing going into it. The only real training is on-the-job experience. Yet, somehow beyond the exhaustion and endless worry, it is awesome. This tiny human suddenly appears, and your whole life changes. I propose there is nothing better in the world, at least from my personal perspective. Others must agree. My measure of proof is that so many people have more than one child. I was blessed with two. A girl and a boy.

I understand everything I do may not help or even be appreciated in the moment. This is frustrating because I want to fix it. I want my kids to be happy. My inability to possess superpowers to make their stress go away stresses me out. The kids are figuring out how to manage their own lives and their own anxiety. They are strong and resilient. We made it through the up-all-night years, the bullying, the teenage drinking and partying, the college years, and exploring the limits years. Honestly, I still worry, but I am more convinced each day that they got this. If at some point they don't, they know I am here. If one day in the very distant future I am not here, I know they have each other and the life skills they need.

The kids are all right.

Robyn: Mentally Speaking

> "Being a mother is learning about strengths
> you didn't know you had and dealing with fears
> you didn't know existed."
> — *Linda Wooten*

My advice to anyone supporting a friend or loved one with anxiety is to be patient. Understand when they push you away or are not responding, they need space. Give it to them, but stay close and involved. Their anxiety is working hard to isolate them, but they really do want to break free and do something with you or talk— they just can't in that moment.

Their battle is personal, and it is difficult for anyone else to relate. It is true you can't fight the battle for them, but your love and support matters. Reinforce and nurture the idea of never giving up or giving in to this illness. Tell them they have the strength to overcome these challenges. Reassure them that no matter how much their anxiety tries to push you away, you are not going anywhere. You love them just the way they are. Make no mistake—anxiety is an illness that can be debilitating. At times, it can make you withdraw and become moody and hard to be around. It compels you to isolate yourself. My daughter, Jennifer ("Walk it Off"), has had to travel down her own path but knows she will always have our love and support when the road gets bumpy. She has blazed her own trail and gained insight into what works for her in managing her mental health.

I first noticed my daughter's anxiety when she was in fifth grade. At the time, she needed to stay at a babysitter's house after school because her dad and I worked full time. The most qualified person we could find to hire was a woman with several children. She was not a clean freak, and my daughter watched the sitter change the babies on the same kitchen counter she served lunch on. This caused Jenn to think about and focus on germs. Her obsession was born. My daughter's compulsions regarding germs continue to this day.

Think about germs; they are literally everywhere, and unless you live in a bubble, you cannot avoid them. Today, she has discovered ways to conquer her fears instead of retreating from the world.

Believe me. Back then, we were aware of her growing anxiety and made arrangements to get her out of the sitter's house as soon as we could. Once she was old enough, we let her stay home alone after school. She would call or text us when she got home. This communication pattern and connection between us continues to this day. It helps us not to worry about each other.

Some of the worry we share is based on her dad's career. While she was growing up, he was in the military and was active during the World Trade Center attacks. He shared the real-world safety issues he dealt with daily, which confirmed for her that true evil exists in the world. Then came his deployments and the ever-present fear for his life and safety. My daughter and I spent many holidays alone worried about him, and while we are closer as a result, worry became an element that was ever-present with us.

It was during this time in her life my daughter's best friend committed suicide. To this very day, it remains a devastating event in her life. They were just kids at thirteen and while he lived in another state at that point, she had just spoken to him and knew he was struggling. He had been recently diagnosed with bipolar disorder. She felt immobilizing guilt. She blamed herself and thought she should have done something more to save him. Of course, that wasn't the case; but to varying degrees, any person in this situation, feels this way. If you take a thirteen-year-old with their level of maturity and development, you can imagine how much more deeply she felt responsible.

We both vividly remember her insisting she had to go to the wake and the burial. The funeral was during a blinding snowstorm, and my car was a little Toyota. My mom instincts were screaming, *no way, we could get killed driving in the storm.* My therapist instincts knew she needed to go to the funeral to get closure. We went, and I hope she got what she needed and came closer to acceptance.

After all these years, I know we did the right thing taking the risk together to drive through the dangerous storm. I desperately wanted to do anything I could to help her. Then began my own anxiety and absolute panic in fearing she would be contemplating a copycat suicide. She became clinically depressed, and I became petrified for her safety and mental health.

During her high school years, tragedy stuck her again and again and again as she lost five friends to fatal car accidents. During the same timeframe, she and I went to Florida often to see my mom who was gravely ill. When my mom passed, we were both heartbroken and struggling. Three years later her beloved grandfather passed away. Losing my dad, her grandfather was our final loss and one that still pains us terribly.

For such a young person, she endured so many losses in just a few years, which compounded her stress, depression, and anxiety. The good news is, love and understanding can heal so much! Even through all the loss and pain, she focused more on appreciation for what she gained by having all those people in her life than what she lost when they passed. All that love shaped her life in positive ways.

171

These deaths caused her to become increasingly anxious about the safety of her dad and me; and us about her. These types of losses really put things in perspective and highlight the value of relationships and family.

In retrospect, it was a tragic time, and she grew up way too fast. Her experiences are now a part of her and have combined together to make her into the woman she is today. They helped her to become strong and compassionate and gave her a drive to help others.

As a therapist, it is unethical and ineffective to provide treatment to your family. I did, however, reach out to a fellow therapist and psychiatrist to get her professional help. She was prescribed medication when she was seventeen, and the therapy and medication helped her a great deal.

Then before we knew it, the time came to decide where to go to college. Was she ready and strong enough to leave home? She had to find the courage within herself and confront her fears about leaving home. Would she feel safe? Could she handle her anxiety on her own? She decided to go away to college. Although she knew she had a loving home and could come back at any time and call whenever she was struggling, it was incredibly hard for her.

The transition to college is a significant life event for so many young adults. It is the first major life change and requires so much strength to adjust and succeed. I, of course, believe this is a time when the support of therapy can be extremely valuable and make the transition easier for just about everyone. Her anxiety, which was accompanied by serious panic attacks, was in many ways, hers and hers alone to manage. That being said, I was still greatly impacted and worried as her mom. The connection between those with lived experience and those with shared experience is deeply linked. As her mother, I feel her pain and anxiety.

To this day, I would have done anything to be able to do more, anything else to ease her suffering. Honestly, I don't actually know what else I could have done, but I think about it often.

In retrospect, I was too protective, which hindered her ability to take control of her anxiety sooner. From a professional viewpoint, when you are too protective of your anxious loved one, it may hinder their sense of control. A sense of control is critical for someone who faces anxiety. Figuring out the balance between stepping in or letting them own and resolve their panic is a fine line and a difficult choice.

How do you know if your involvement is too much or not enough? It is a tough question. As a mother, I believe you can never love your child too much or do too much to ease their pain. The most you can hope for as a parent is that your child grows up relatively unscathed. Anxiety, as long as it is managed, is an obstacle, yes, but it is not insurmountable. People with anxiety disorders can and do lead successful and happy lives. I see it every day through my daughter's eyes and in my patients' successes.

As a licensed clinician, I work with patients on becoming aware of their anxiety or impending panic attacks…to identify any precipitating factors. The point being to assist them to develop insight and make their anxiety their own, to take control. Once it isn't just some random thing happening *to* them, it becomes manageable. Once you gain knowledge or awareness, you can work on a cognitive level (i.e. CBT therapy). Dealing intellectually about an emotional illness has very real medical overtones.

Clinicians support people to pace their expectations. Most people want a quick fix, but by the time they engage in therapy, they already have serious symptoms that have gone untreated for a long time. They are starting from a point of feeling immobilized. The most important first course of action is to begin to see they may not be in control at that moment, but they can and will be in control with hard work, perseverance, and a belief in themselves and the process. As a mother and a clinician, I wish I had a magic wand to cure everyone of their anxiety and depression, but since I don't, I guess we all have to rely on love, compassion, and treatment.

Traci: Inside Out

> "The love you give away to the world
> will be reflected on your children,
> and their children after them."
> —*Emily Ley*

I have always known there was something different about my son,
Sam ("Liar, Liar, My Mind is on Fire").

He could play for hours by himself in an imaginary world. It
took an incredible amount of prodding and pleading with him to
get him to share any part of his world with me. He was fascinated by
letters at a very early age and developed the ability to read before he
had conversational speech skills. While grocery shopping, heads
turned as my 20-month-old baby recited the words written on the
walls in each department.

He was brilliant. He put on an amazing show for anyone and
everyone watching when it came to letters and words. When he
entered pre-school, he wowed his classmates and teachers with his
aptitude for reading and ability to memorize books that were read in

class. I was sure I had a genius for a child!

Then the day came when I pulled up to pick him up from pre-school and noticed something bothersome.

The entire class was outside on the playground, and they were chasing each other, playing ball, and doing all of the things you'd expect children do on the playground. Then there sat Sam, under a tree, spinning a leaf between his fingers.

It was odd. Why was he not playing with the other kids?

He looked content. He didn't seem upset at all. He actually appeared to be very happy, in his own little world, spinning his leaf, just like he would at home. But there weren't other kids his age at home to play with. Shouldn't he be enjoying playing with the rest of his class?

I asked his teacher about it. She immediately shared she also had concerns regarding Sam's lack of social interaction. Unexpectedly, and seemingly out of the blue, we were trying to figure out where to bring our son and figure out what we were even looking for by "testing him."

We called early intervention services. They came to our house, talked to us and to Sam, and deemed him ineligible for services. He was able to make eye contact, answer questions, and read on a first-grade level at the age of four. They were not concerned. We were incredibly relieved, our prior panic seeming silly. Sam was fine, a bit unique, but fine.

Our relief was short lived.

Later that year, Sam displayed increasingly concerning repetitive behaviors as well as frequent temper tantrums, particularly when his routine was disrupted. Back to square one. We got more testing and another opinion. Upon completion of more extensive psychological testing, Sam was diagnosed with Asperger's Syndrome.

What was that? I had never heard of it, so I began researching it. I felt like I was reading an exact description written about Sam. Now what? How do we help him? What does he need? How will this impact his life? His future?

We dedicated the next few years to creating a structured routine for Sam. We read books and discussed friendship, emotions, appropriate behavior, and empathy on a constant loop with him. We enrolled him in drama classes to learn social interaction skills. He was kind to his two younger brothers. He attended school where he achieved exceptional grades and made and maintained friendships with his classmates. Once again, we were relieved and overjoyed. Sam had managed to overcome so many of the obstacles we had once been so concerned about. We were so relieved.

Ten years later, from all outward appearances, Sam was still doing exceptionally well. His aptitude for letters and words had developed into a passion for writing, composing, and performing music.

During high school, Sam joined several bands and was actively involved in the drama department. From the outside looking in, it appeared as if he had overcome the obstacles that had been so concerning in his early childhood. However, we started to notice more and more things that individually would have been minor, but collectively, they were not. Concern slowly crept back into our lives.

On stage, when performing with a band, or in a play, Sam exuded confidence. He sold his part, hook, line, and sinker. He never disappointed an audience. What he was feeling on the inside was never shown to the audience. All the anxiety and worry was hidden, but as soon as the show was over, Sam was gone. It was like a disappearing act done by a master magician. He would slip right out the back door and never look back.

I remember countless times searching for him after a performance and pleading with him to come back inside. Just for a few minutes. Our friends and family all wanted to see him and congratulate him on his performance. They had come to support him. Reluctantly, he would come back inside. He'd stay for as little time as possible, looking uncomfortable, his eyes on the door. He'd answer every compliment with a tight "thank you" and every question with a "yes" or "no." He'd thank people for coming. But his heart wasn't in it, and he clearly wanted nothing more than to be a million miles away. Or at least back at home, holed up in his room with his music.

I never understood this. He had just sung at the top of his lungs on stage in front of hundreds of people. Why did he act so oddly afterwards? He clearly loved performing. Something in the aftermath of a show, when the interactions turned unplanned, unscripted, and unrehearsed, was deeply upsetting for him. I had no idea at the time about any of the paralyzing anxiety he now describes feeling when interacting with people after his shows, even with his friends and family.

Sam has never liked to ask for help. He didn't talk about these things, ever, even to me. The only glimpses we would get into what was going on with Sam was through his original songs he wrote. The intense and vivid descriptions of emotions were alarming.

I would listen to the lyrics of a song, sometimes ones he showed me and sometimes ones I heard drifting out from underneath his closed bedroom door. I would ask him about the song, about what made him think about that in particular when he had written it. He would usually reluctantly tell me at least a bit about what he was thinking and feeling at that point. This worked well when he was younger and living at home, but all too soon, Sam left for college to pursue a degree in music.

At home, I thought about him constantly and hoped he would do well in college. He was free to (mostly) focus on his music. I thought he would be able to find like-minded people with similar interests and develop some confidence in his skills. For the first year, everything seemed to be going okay. Then again, from the outside, things with Sam usually seemed to be okay.

As fall rolled around in his sophomore year, Sam was excited to get back to school. He was moving off campus and would be living on his own, away from the hubbub of the dorms. It was a very short time before I knew once again something was very wrong. This time, Sam was diagnosed with generalized anxiety disorder and depression. I felt blindsided. Sam had always struggled to fit in with his peers. It was hard for him to connect. He preferred to do things by himself. That was just Sam.

We had no idea he had been suffering debilitating social anxiety and having panic attacks for years. As a mom, my first thought was, *what did I do wrong? How could I possibly have missed this? What could I have done to help him? What happened to my once vibrant, animated, happy, motivated, self-content little boy?*

I was at a loss for what to do to help him. How could I help him? We would speak on the phone once or twice a week while he was away at school, but my maternal instinct wanted to call several times a day. I worried about him all day, every day. It consumed me.

When he did call me, my initial response was never relief; it was panic. Sometimes when we spoke, Sam appeared to be on top of the world. He seemed happy and fulfilled. Everything seemed to be looking up. The next call, his world was falling apart...like it was over and couldn't be fixed.

His panic attacks became more frequent and now, most of the time, he was unable to identify what triggered them. They were getting out of control. Knowing all of this was going on with him and not knowing how to help him was the biggest struggle I have faced as a parent. When Sam was younger, he and I could sit, talk, and work through his fears. It was never easy, but at least it was possible. I saw him everyday, and I was able to help him. I could assess if he was truly okay. As I heard him playing his guitar in his room, I could reassure myself he was okay, that we were getting there, that he was going to be fine.

Now, it was my job to let go so that he could build confidence in his own ability to live life, without Mommy walking him through every step. If I let go, could he handle all this on his own? It was a terrifying decision. Sam did make it through college and as an adult, continues to gain insight about himself and how to manage his anxiety.

As his mom, my instincts are to rush in and help him through the difficult times. I want to protect him. I'm slowly accepting he can only grow when he works through each situation in his own way and in his own time. Each panic attack or period of depression he comes out on the other side of convinces us both that he can do this. He's gaining the skills he needs to manage his anxiety and depression, a little at a time. I'm learning to control my panic and urge to shield him from everything, a little at a time.

When he calls me now, I no longer panic.

When he calls me now, we talk…sometimes about things that are bothering him, but more often, about the ways he is learning to live with his mental-health challenges. The most exciting conversations for me are when he calls to tell me about how he is conquering each new situation one day at a time, without me holding his hand. My little boy is truly a man…a man I am proud of and one I know will be just fine.

Liz: Free Hugs

"A mother is the truest friend we have, when
trials heavy and sudden fall upon us; when adversity takes
the place of prosperity; when friends who rejoice with us in our
sunshine, desert us when troubles thicken around us, still will
she cling to us, and endeavor by her kind precepts and
counsels to dissipate the clouds of darkness and
cause peace to return to our hearts."
—*Washington Irving*

For over thirty-five years, I have worked as a nurse in orthopedics, oncology, critical care, emergency, and surgical medicine. Professionally, I manage a great deal of stress, especially when taking care of critical care patients.

I am the youngest of four children. My oldest sister is fourteen years older than me. My parents were well into their thirties when I was born, and by the time I came along, Dad was already in failing health. I was Daddy's little girl, and I wanted him to be healthy. By the age of eight, I knew that wasn't going to happen. I decided I wanted to become a nurse.

I spent my eighteenth birthday in the intensive care unit with Dad, who was in critical condition. I slept in a chair in the waiting room for several nights. I wanted to be there and needed to be there, as I was already a nurse, and my family was depending on me for answers and "to be strong." I held my emotions in and didn't share how bad he was in an effort to protect my grandmother who had already buried one son during World War II. My mother constantly reminded me that if Grandma lost another son, it would kill her. I was very close with my grandmother and wanted to prevent her from experiencing more pain or loss. Dad did eventually improve and go home, and I did my best to keep him as healthy as possible.

My mother and I were a different story. I don't recall us ever having a close or supportive relationship. There were so many things I wanted to share and talk to her about. I longed for my mom's advice and guidance. Since there was a void, I learned to depend on myself and became very independent. I had no idea how stressful life as an adult could be as I got married, divorced, had children, and experienced heartbreaking loss. In just a six-year period, I had my first son, lost my second son, lost my dad, had my daughter, moved three times, lost my mother, and got divorced. I was stressed, exhausted, depressed, and just plain sad and lonely. Stress was everywhere…at home, at work, and in my heart, but I had two young kids to take care of.

I took my kids to counseling after the divorce, found them a great after-school program, and maintained a relationship with their father. I wanted to be sure they knew we both loved them, and nothing was their fault. I had it all covered.

So, I was shocked and upset as I began to understand both of my children had major anxiety disorders.

I realized my son, at the age of six, had experienced the same losses and major life changes I had. Knowing this, I had a heightened awareness and did everything I could think of to give him a stable home. He still struggled. I could not commit to plans because the slightest change would send him into a frenzy, resulting in temper tantrums. He had a stubborn streak, and his personality was similar to his father's. This made our relationship tricky at first but then stronger as he got older. Being so similar to his dad also strained their relationship, as they collided over so many issues.

My son, Joe, although very intelligent, struggled in school. He was labeled as an "underachiever" as he procrastinated and managed to only meet the minimum requirements to pass. Then he would frantically cram for exams. I learned I need to be very thoughtful and structured when I talk with him because it is difficult to know what will trigger an angry response. I feel like I am walking on eggshells every time I communicate with him. Joe feels extreme stress and anxiety at the smallest adjustments in his life or environment. He experiences the world as very chaotic. He calls me in distress over everything from technology issues with his phone to stressing over when he can't find something. I just couldn't understand "what the big deal was." Now, I realize the big deal is he needs to have a sense of control. So, I consciously remind myself to be patient and remain calm in his moments of stress.

My daughter, Kristen (Wall of Doom) is an overachiever and puts incredible stress on herself to succeed at everything. In the rare instance she got a grade below a 90, she was devastated. She is a people pleaser and wants to save the world. When she was in high school, I began to realize this drive towards perfection was taking a toll on her.

There is nothing more heartbreaking and more scary for a mother than picking up the phone and hearing your daughter hysterically crying on the phone, inaudibly sobbing to the point you are thinking she was physically hurt, or someone has died. The phone calls came more often in her freshman and sophomore years of college. She called a couple of times a week, upset about her grades and her fear of failing. Her lowest grade was a B (she graduated with honors and a 3.7 grade point average). Kristen was constantly over-whelmed with the amount of work assigned by her professors. We developed a routine. I would calm her down, and then we would break down everything that was due into smaller, actionable steps. What reading is due first? Then what paper?

My daughter tried medication, but it didn't help. She tried coun-seling, meditation, and exercise. I visited her in college often. She adopted a cat and had it classified as an emotional support animal. She selected a blind, old cat, which goes along with her personality of trying to save people/animals. Anxiety during her senior year in college reached an all-time high when her high school sweetheart died. She had always believed they would get married. She was depressed, and I feared all her hard work would be for nothing. I was afraid she would need to come home and not graduate. She managed to work through her grief with the support of her friends and family. She was accepted to a graduate school program through New York State and started teaching in the city.

Her first year of teaching was strenuous. I received multiple calls from her as she became overwhelmed by grading tests and papers while also completing her graduate school classes. She called often crying about her students because she was impacted by the struggles they were facing in their lives. I continued to break down tasks into smaller ones, prioritizing with her what needs to be done, and also supporting her desire to change the world without sacrificing herself in the process. I have witnessed growth and maturity in the last year, and the calls are fewer and farther apart. Although she still procrasti-nates, it doesn't cause the level of anxiety it used to.

It was a difficult learning process for me to take life and stress in stride. I adjusted over time because my initial reaction to my children's stress was: Life is tough so suck it up, buttercup! It didn't resonate with me why people stressed over what I considered regular life until it was my child in distress. I will always be supportive of my children and be there for them. The one thing I longed for my whole life was a hug from my mother reassuring me everything would be okay. Yet it was the one thing I never got. As long as I am alive, I will be there for my children smothering them with hugs and anything else they need.

Part IV

THE ROAD AHEAD:
BUCKLE UP, IT MIGHT BE A LITTLE BUMPY

Anxiety Disorders: Nicole

There is not a single type of anxiety. There are probably thousands of "kinds" of anxiety in the current best understanding of anxiety disorders. Mental-health professionals use a book called the *Diagnostic and Statistical Manual of Mental Disorders* (DSM, referenced earlier) as a guide to diagnosing psychiatric disorders. It classifies anxiety disorders into nine distinct disorders—that's if you don't count the ones that exclusively apply to kids and focus only on pure anxiety disorders.

Although it sounds (and in some ways is) complex, a lot of the disorders are familiar to all of us. Many of these diagnoses have become terms commonly used in conversation. I have mixed feelings about this. I love to hear people being open about their mental health and feeling free to speak without fear of stigma. However, when clinical terms are used casually in everyday conversation, they come to represent one thing in everyday discussions and another to patients and their doctors. In the normal vs. pathologic anxiety discussion, this can be a contributing factor in miscommunications. One person is trying to open up about their experience of a debilitating anxiety disorder and the other person, meaning no harm or ill intent, instead of seeing this as a significant disclosure someone is trying to share asking follow up questions or offering help, shares her own story about having to give a presentation last week, which "felt" stressful. For our purposes here, I'm speaking entirely about clinical disorders.

With no further fanfare, I present to you, a brief summary of the DSM's nine recognized anxiety disorders:

Generalized Anxiety Disorder

This is the prototypical "anxious person." They're worried about their work performance, their cat, their relationships, fires, floods, or natural disasters, and even serial killers. They will worry about whatever and usually all of the above. It's not something they're able to easily control or rationalize away, and it's disruptive to their lives.

This is the most common anxiety disorder. Most people who are diagnosed with one of the more specific disorders will struggle with this at some time as well—defined by excessive and irrational worrying about many things over the course of months to years. The chronic activation of stress hormones tends to lead to a variety of cognitive (concentration problems, irritability) or physical (problems sleeping, muscle tension, restlessness) symptoms as well. The physical symptoms can be severe but nonspecific and often aren't connected to the anxiety behaviors (by the patient or their doctor) until the anxiety is recognized and treated. Then the rest of the symptoms seem to magically vanish (personal experience).

Panic Disorder

Experiences vary quite a bit—defined by a feeling of intense fear that comes on suddenly and inappropriately (when there is not really anything to actually be afraid of). These attacks are usually accompanied by a variety of physical symptoms to add to the sufferer's concern that they may actually be dying, including heart palpitations, feeling short of breath, choking, dizziness, sweating, and nausea. The physical symptoms can play a prominent role in the episodes and are often the first thing mentioned to healthcare providers.

To add to the chaos, when people get scared, they breathe too fast. If you breathe too fast for more than a few minutes, it messes with the oxygen and carbon dioxide levels in your body. That's not generally actually dangerous in this context; if nothing else is physically wrong, worst-case scenario, you cause yourself to pass out briefly, in which case your body will be able to start breathing normally again without your pesky brain in the way. Everything will quickly right itself. But it feels pretty horrible in the moment (also personal experience).

Agoraphobia
This is basically a side effect of severe panic disorder. People get into a cycle where they have panic attacks in certain situations and in an attempt to avoid the attacks, start avoiding those situations. This is an understandable response, but it can spiral and progress from things like avoiding the building where you first had a panic attack, to things like avoiding being in a car ever, or refusing to leave home at all (which is isolating and concerning).

Social Anxiety Disorder
This is a fear of being embarrassed or humiliated in front of others. Most people have this fear to some extent. Humans are built to be incredibly sensitive to social rejection. It crosses into concerning when it interferes with your ability to go to work or school, superficially interact with people in your day-to-day life, or form and maintain meaningful relationships throughout your life.

Specific Phobia
This tends to be the anxiety disorder most often represented in the media. A phobia is basically a very intense fear of one thing. It happens every time you encounter that one thing and generally leads to a decent amount of distress and avoidance. This isn't someone who dislikes bugs. To qualify as a true phobia, the fear has to be

severe enough to disrupt your day-to-day life. For example, not liking elevators or being a little anxious in them? Normal. Being so afraid to get in an elevator that you're taking the stairs to your office on the fourteenth floor every day despite the fact that it adds half an hour to your day, you hate it, and you arrive sweaty and gross? Not normal.

Substance-Induced Anxiety Disorder
A bit of an outlier, but for the sake of thoroughness, this is when someone is very anxious as the direct result of a substance. This can apply either to medical medications with anxiety as a side effect (steroids can sometimes do this, for one) or to illegal drugs that are also commonly known to cause anxiety, such as cocaine. When the substance goes away, the anxiety goes away.

Anxiety Disorder Caused by a General Medical Condition
Very similar to the last disorder with the distinction, the anxiety is caused by a medical condition. It boils down to the same thing. There's a chemical in your body at levels that are abnormal and causing anxiety; the distinction is that it's a chemical your body is making, not one that you're ingesting. The prototypical example is an overactive thyroid. Fix the medical problem; fix the anxiety.

Other Disorders
Because we are in this deep, and I am unable to resist, let's look at a few disorders highly associated with anxiety disorders.

<u>The (Exclusively) Kids' Ones</u>

Separation anxiety is an excessive anxiety about being away from home or caregivers in a child who has passed the age where this is developmentally appropriate. It most commonly tends to manifest as school refusal or avoidance in elementary school children.

Selective mutism is a phenomenon that occurs more commonly than you would think where a child refuses to speak in certain situations despite being capable of speaking and often observed to be speaking comfortably in other situations. Despite the inability to speak not being a physical barrier, it's also not simply a matter of will or defiance and generally responds to treatment.

Obsessive-Compulsive Disorders

The obsessive-compulsive disorders (OCDs) are, in my belief, some of the most commonly misunderstood mental illnesses. There is a milder form of illness with some similar-looking symptoms referred to as *obsessive compulsive personality disorder* that is more common than OCD and adds to some of the confusion.

OCD is a disorder characterized by obsessions and compulsions. Obsessions are repetitive and intrusive thoughts that are generally very distressing. Obsessions can take different forms and look different in different people, but they are often terrifying and distressing thoughts—part of the reason I think OCD deserves a mention in any discussion of anxiety disorders.

As a result of these obsessions, people feel compelled to perform repetitive behaviors known as *compulsions*. This tends to look like the patients have one or multiple obsessions causing them a great amount of anxiety and distress, which they attempt to mitigate by spending a large portion of their day performing compulsive behaviors. A prototypical example would be someone who is very afraid of germs and needs to wash his hands three times before he eats or touches his face and after every single time he touches a door handle. These people believe if they skip doing this even one time, they will get deathly ill and likely die. It's not a rational belief, and the patients are usually aware of that, but they still feel like they have to do it.

Body dysmorphic disorder is a form of OCD in which someone is preoccupied with a small or imagined defect in their physical appearance to the point it causes them a great deal of distress on a daily basis.

Hoarding disorder also falls into this category. Hoarding is defined as accumulating items that will likely not have much utility in the future in a compulsive manner. Typically, patients are unable to let go of any of the items once they have them and even thinking about doing so causes incredible anxiety.

Trichotillomania is compulsively pulling out your own hair. It can be from any part of your body and is often a response to stress but has reached a point where it feels impossible to control or resist. Similarly, *excoriation* is basically the same emotional pattern, but manifests as picking at skin to the point of injury rather than pulling out hair.

Somatic Symptom Disorders

The term you've probably heard is *hypochondriac*. These folks have a lot of anxiety and persistent concerns that there is something medically wrong with them, despite evidence to the contrary. In the case of *somatic symptom disorder*, this is generally paying a lot of attention to physical sensations within the body and having anxiety that either normal physiologic things (cuts or minor bruising, fatigue, occasional headaches) or minor symptoms (chronic low back pain, occasional coughing, diarrhea sometimes) are signs of severe medical disease. *Illness anxiety disorder* is a similar persistent fear of being sick, but without any physical complaints or symptoms.

Finally, within this group of disorders is one that I, as a doctor, have always found to be fascinating: *functional neurological symptom disorder*. This disorder is when someone has neurological symptoms (like weakness, numbness, vision problems, or sensory deficits), but after appropriate medical testing, do not have any medical or neurological conditions causing those symptoms. The patients are not faking their symptoms or misrepresenting their experience. They actually cannot see or cannot move their arms; it's just not a physical issue as much as a mental one. It's a hard diagnosis to make and one patients have a hard time hearing. It can come across to the patient as the doctor saying the symptoms aren't real, when the truth is, the symptoms are real. The cause is just something we can't see on labs or point to on a picture of the brain. The symptoms tend to wax and wane but like most disorders, get worse under stress.

I end this section with this group of disorders because they are near and dear to my heart and, really, to what we hope to accomplish with this book. I was a severe hypochondriac until at least college. And although relatively rare (or at least) rarely diagnosed, I saw functional neurologic disorders during my medical training, and it was one of the places where I found insight and understanding to make some of the most crucial differences in patient outcomes. For patients who are able to accept the diagnosis beyond "not real symptoms" (usually aided by incredible and empathetic providers who take a lot of time to explain and answer questions), the prognosis is often good. With therapy, sometimes anxiety medications, and time, their symptoms generally resolve. When symptoms recur, patients are able to recognize what is happening, seek appropriate care, and wait for them to pass at home.

When patients aren't able to get to this point, it can lead to strings of ER visits and hospital admissions spanning years, with the patients being continually anxious about their symptoms and upset by medicine's inability to "find the problem." On the other side, medical providers are increasingly frustrated about the symptoms driving the repeated ER visits not being "real" and failing to connect with these patients or explain what they think is going on in a way the patient is able to understand (and hopefully come to accept).

The bigger takeaway with these disorders (and the intersection of physical and mental health, in general) is there is so much we still don't entirely understand about the inner workings of the brain and nervous system and how it relates to our overall health. In functional neurologic disorders, something in the brain is causing real symptoms, yet it's not a problem we know how to find in a way we can point to on a screen. Similarly, there are new discoveries, it seems weekly, that relate things like bacteria in our guts to depression or chronic inflammatory disorders. We know chronic mental illness does, over years, cause changes in brain structure that we can see on brain scans, but what's actually happening on a day-to-day basis to make this happen over time is still poorly understood. There's so much we don't yet understand about how the brain works or the exact links between all of the hormones, molecules, and thousands of genes that interact to form our physical and mental health. What we do know is that mental illness can be linked to specific disruptions in chemicals in the brain that can be effectively treated by both medications and therapy in a way that allows people to suffer less distress related to their anxiety, and we're continually working to expand our treatment options for these patients with research to develop more effective medications and therapies for patients who continue to suffer.

Common Coping Strategies: What Works and What Doesn't

Let's dive in and start with the bad (or unhealthy) coping strategies. We talk about them here not as suggestions, but because they are common themes you've read throughout the memoirs. To be clear, these are things we do not recommend as ways of dealing with anxiety or any other mental illness, partially because they may cause long-term harm but mostly, because they don't work. Research has shown us these things generally worsen mental-health outcomes rather than improve them, but unfortunately, since they sometimes bring small improvements in mood for the moment at the expense of tomorrow, next week, or next year, they remain common among people who are struggling to manage their illness.

Self-Medicating/Substance Use

Self-medicating is a real and often overused coping mechanism for millions of people. It is hard to recognize and even harder to admit. Self-medicating is using alcohol and/or drugs to cope with stress or depression. Alcohol is a socially accepted commodity, which has been around for centuries, and there is tons of research and data on its use and effects on health.

And then there is marijuana. Science, cultural norms, and public perception are all still evolving in the United States. Each state decides for itself about laws governing marijuana use for both recreational and medical use. There are valid perspectives on all sides of the discussion regarding the positive and negative effects of this drug in the treatment of medical issues including mental health and anxiety disorders. Regardless, it is worth considering if marijuana or alcohol alone can solve deep-rooted psychological issues that might benefit more from engaging in cognitive behavioral therapy.

Positive Coping strategies

Coping skills or strategies are constructive ways to reduce stress. They are specific actions that can be taken to reduce, minimize, or tolerate stress and anxiety. They can be behavioral or psychological. Basically, they are ways to face or manage stress and anxiety. Below are some of the ones that worked for those of us who shared our stories in this book. We are not presenting them as scientifically or medically researched or proven. They simply helped us, and they might help you, your child, family member, friend, coworker, student, employee, or neighbor…really, anyone looking for more calm in their lives. We summarized them and listed them for easy reference. The secret to success is different for each one of us. So, try new things, and you might be surprised what works for you or a loved one. You might fall in love with a new hobby, activity, or pet. Trial and error and action are the keys. Good luck!

Faith and Prayers

My mom believes there is something out there beyond her control, be it faith, fate, or destiny. For her, believing there is a higher power protecting her and those she loves alleviated stress by reducing her doubt, anger, fear, grief, and confusion. It offered her a path to tolerance and forgiveness. It offered hope. She found saying a prayer alone or with someone else, going to church, or tuning into a religious radio station brought her a sense of calm and strength. She practiced praying and reading her *Bible* daily until her dementia took away her ability to read. I am not overly religious, but I do pray on occasion as a form of recognizing and expressing gratitude for what I have or to ask for protection for those I love.

Music

I believe music is powerful. It speaks to our emotions, brings out laughter, fears, sadness, love, hope, and evokes a connection. Music expresses feelings we are both aware of and unaware of while entertaining and distracting us.

Music is at the center of Sam's world and career. He has been in bands and writing songs since middle school. He went to college for sound engineering and works in a music store. Music is his passion and refuge. Music is also part of Jenny's world and has been an outlet for her emotions since she was a teenager. It is a universal experience on some level for music to connect us to our emotions. It offers a pathway to get lost in it and be distracted. It also brings people together in many ways. Nicole and her friends enjoy karaoke after a long, stressful week. For them, singing out loud and spending time together is a fun, social outlet for their emotions and stress.

You know: "Sing, sing a song. Make it simple, to last your whole life long. Don't worry that it's not good enough for anyone to hear. Just sing, sing a song."—*Shirley Bassey*

Employee Assistance Program (EAP)

Wendy, Rachel, and I, as human resource professionals, recommend if your employer has an EAP and you are struggling with stress and anxiety, balance in your life, feeling sad, or dealing with grief, that you give them a call. EAPs offer assessments, short-term counseling, referrals, and follow-up services to employees and their family members who have emotional, personal, or work-related issues. This is an employee benefit paid for by your employer and is confidential. They give you a referral and, in some areas, tele-health services are available. The better care you take of yourself, the better you can handle stress or help those around you. EAPs also offer health and wellness programs to support you with healthy eating, weight loss, financial counseling, legal advice, addiction services, and smoking cessation. It is free and confidential.

Coloring

My mother, Carolann, colors all day long, every day. When she is concentrating on her coloring, she forgets the terror of not remembering where she is or much about who she is, which is very stressful. I have found coloring at any age can reduce stress, relieve anxiety, exercise your brain, spark creativity, and increase self-awareness and mindfulness. It is like taking an adult timeout. Adult coloring can be an alternative to meditation as a form of mindfulness. Taking a little time for yourself allows you to block out distractions, take a break from critical thinking, and ignite creativity. After disconnecting from the world even for short periods of time, I begin to feel refreshed and energized. Coloring is an easy and inexpensive activity you can do alone, with your kids, or with friends. Color your world beautiful.

Arts and Crafts

My mom has always been creative and loved to crochet, paint, sew, needlepoint, and knit. She taught these skills to my sister and me. Then she taught her grandkids. When my children were younger, they spent hours with my mom doing these hobbies. They loved it. They had fun, it was relaxing and, in the end, they made something. All good things. Maybe crocheting, which seems to be an "older" person thing today, will make a comeback and "blanket" the world with a sense of calm. In the past few months, since the beginning of the 2020 pandemic, I have seen sewing make a comeback as people everywhere are making face masks for their own personal protection and as gifts for our courageous health-care workers. The talent and creativity emerging have been fun and impressive to see. "Old Fashioned" skills like sewing will never be obsolete. Why not give it a try?

Journaling

Nicole, James, and Jenny all find journaling to be something they enjoy that helps them have quiet time to process their thoughts. By writing them down, they can acknowledge the distressing thoughts and then let them go. It also gives them time to reflect about the people and things in their lives they are grateful for and enjoy. Journaling presents an opportunity to clear thoughts and process emotions from stressful or traumatic events while bringing unhealthy patterns of behavior to your awareness. Journaling is a purposeful way to think, feel, discover, plan, and dream. Jenny learned this skill as a teenager while hospitalized, and it continues to be an activity she finds helpful and relaxing. If you are interested, there are sites and blogs about the different types of journaling. It is a way to be reflective and examine your thoughts and feelings privately...a way to truly connect with yourself. You may like what you discover.

Jogging

Nicole and Emily find jogging helps them to stay on track. There is something magical about jogging and listening to an audio book that provides an exhilarating and healthy escape. The rhythm of jogging, combined with having your mind occupied, is a great combination for Nicole. Exercise of any kind helps control anxiety. Endorphins are released from the brain while exercising. For some of us, exercise is a powerful tool in fighting anxiety. I have friends who are avid runners and say it is therapy for the soul. They find it to be rejuvenating, and it brings them inner peace. Although I acknowledge there is something to it, I have to admit I am still at the walking phase myself.

Housework/Chores

Wendy finds getting up and doing routine housework, like washing dishes, brings her a sense of calm. I find de-cluttering or cleaning out a closet or room to be a good distraction that offers a sense of accomplishment and order once completed. I honestly wish I found cleaning worked as a better coping tool for me because my house could use a whole lot more of it. But hey, like I said, not everything works for everyone.

Exercise

For James, exercise is a powerful way to manage his anxiety. It seems to be a natural antidepressant for him.

Finding some form of exercise you love or at least don't hate is important for your overall health. It is not easy, but the benefits clearly outweigh the effort. Join a gym, ride a bike, join a softball or basketball league, hire a personal trainer, dance, swim, garden, mow the lawn, hike, or rock climb. I understand and appreciate it is difficult for some of us (myself included) to really get into these activities but keep trying. A body in motion stays in motion.

Walking

Walking is so simple. Almost anyone can do it anywhere, anytime. It is good for your mind and body. Jennifer discovered this in the middle of a panic attack. There does seem to be a connection between movement and reducing anxiety. By exercising or at least moving when you are stressed, you burn energy, and the activity supports your body to feel better which in turn makes your mind feel better. Jennifer found another benefit of walking was the increased production of carbon dioxide, which enabled her to breathe better while also increasing her blood flow, thus, combining together to reduce her anxiety. The experience of walking, especially if you can get outside, also offers a distraction from your anxious thoughts without you having to purposefully refocus your thoughts. It just happens. As you take in the sights and smells and feel the fresh air on your face, your mind takes notice of all these things. You may not realize it, but your brain has to process all you are seeing and doing, which reduces your focus and concentration on your stressful thoughts. Try it. Walk. Breathe. Walk alone and enjoy the peace. Walk and listen to music or an audio book. Walk your dog. Walk with a friend. Walk with a group of friends. Just walk.

Deep Breathing

We all breathe. It is the "how" we breathe that makes the difference. Sam uses a focus on breathing to bring a sense of calm and control to his life when he feels a panic attack coming on. Breathing is an essential tool he uses to manage his anxiety. Deep, intentional breathing can calm the mind and the body. Just a few long, deep, intentional breaths can make the difference between control and the onset of a full-blown panic attack. Air is free; breathe more.

Yoga

I recently started taking yoga classes at a studio in town. The combination of mindfulness, stretching, and balance is great (especially for this old body). My anxiety causes tension resulting in muscle pain. The benefits of yoga are really adding up. In class the other day, we did a breathing exercise I found very interesting. Sit relaxed and take a deep breath in through your nose for four seconds and picture your breath as a deep gold color. Then exhale with your eyes closed and picture your breath being released and forming a protective cloud around you. Repeat until you achieve the imagery of a large cloud surrounding you. Inside, you are relaxed and safe. Clear your mind and just focus. Why not try a few classes with different instructors? You can even take classes in person or on line. Each class and instructor is very different, but I bet there is one for you out there somewhere. *Namaste.*

Cook a Meal

After a long, stressful day, I discovered I love cooking. I was shocked because I always believed I wasn't a very good cook. But I have been ordering fresh meal kits for over a year now. Everything you need to cook a fresh, healthy meal comes in a box to your door. There is no need to figure out what to cook, no need to go to the store, and no need to look up recipes. It is all just magically there. I put on some music and follow the easy steps and bam, dinner is ready! The simplicity of following the steps and ending up with a delicious meal is soothing. This has been a lifesaver the past few months as the coronavirus hit us all. As of this writing, I have been taking care of my 83-year-old dad, who is home on hospice, and I am trying to protect him by following the stay-at-home orders and not going out to stores. We get our box of ingredients every week and enjoy great meals in our bubble of isolation. (At least until this pandemic is under control.) You, too, may have some hidden culinary skills. You won't know until you try. Start a cooking group (perhaps virtual for now) and get together and make new recipes. Please send me some of your favorites so I can try them. I particularly like Italian, Mexican, seafood, and anything with guacamole in it.

Mindfulness

Mindfulness is simply quieting your mind. I recently downloaded the app, CALM. I have been trying to practice being present and aware of where I am and what I am doing without being reactive or overwhelmed by what's going on around me. Mindfulness is something everyone can practice. Mindfulness can be done informally anywhere and anytime for short or long periods of time. There are numerous apps out there you can download on your phone or computer. Give them a try. You never know, it could improve your overall physical and mental health.

My son and I both feel that mindfulness is like taking your brain for a virtual walk. Like our bodies, our minds need time to recover after a difficult work out. It is a way to "walk" it off, relax, take a deep breath, and be fully present. Notice what you see, smell, feel, and hear. Be in the moment as you gain insight and nurture yourself. Even a few seconds or minutes is enough. Don't over think it. It isn't the formal practice of meditation, and you don't need sneakers.

Find Your People: Support System

All of us need and want friends and to fit in and be accepted. It is a basic human need. When you find people who really "get you," you feel it deep in your soul. If you have them in your life, let them know how much you appreciate them. If you don't, keep looking. They are out there.

The friends we choose to spend our time with can make our anxiety better or worse. Because anxiety creates self-doubt and decreases self-confidence, it can be easier to keep friends who do not always treat us with kindness and respect. Be aware, because they can significantly impact your opinion of yourself and your ability to cope. Don't settle. Be choosy. You are worth it.

If you can't be yourself or honest about your feelings and struggles with your friends, it might be time to look for new friends. If they make comments or off-handed remarks that make you feel uncomfortable or doubt yourself, it is definitely time to move on. Breanna found the courage to let go of toxic friends, which positively changed her life. We grow, we change. Seek people who fit your future, friends who support your dreams and goals, and friends who believe in you.

Stay Connected

Anxiety has the power to propel us to retreat and to want to be alone. Sometimes we just need down time, time to rest and reset, which is normal and fine, but resist doing this for too long. Before you know it, time has passed, and you have isolated yourself. After a day or two, force yourself to reach out and call or text a friend. Getting together even just for a walk or cup of coffee can be a healthy, positive way to reconnect. If you are thinking of expanding, adding, or changing your circle of friends, consider joining a gym, a club, or a church. Take a class, volunteer in your community, or go to a local library's book club. There are good people in the world. Go find them. You have a lot to offer the world.

Pets

For many of us, our pets are important members of our families. This is true for Nicole. She loves her cats, Houdini and Blane (the boys). They bring her comfort. One of the amazing qualities about animals is their ability to give unconditional love and acceptance. They reduce loneliness, improve moods, and don't judge you. They offer an unlimited supply of entertainment and a playful distraction. Animals can offer a sense of safety and security. When Nicole cuddles her cats, she finds their purring to be soothing. I know for a fact when she walks in the door, and they run to greet her, it makes her day. I have two cats, Brix and Pedro, who give me lots of love. My cats bring me a sense of calm.

Most people are either cat people or dog people. So, let's talk dogs. Dogs are wonderful, loyal companions and offer a sense of protection. They are great walking buddies, helping you stay active. James has a dog, Thor, which he adopted in college. Thor has survived many college roommates and a few fraternity parties. When James is lonely or sad, they go for a long walk to the beach or dog park.

If you have been considering getting a pet, stop into a local shelter and see what happens. You could walk away with a new friend or maybe you will decide to volunteer.

Acting

Here's a unique option, but hey, you never know. Jenny found a passion and a career in acting. Acting offers her an outlet to channel her feelings, emotions, and experiences from life. It is a way to express herself while drawing upon the benefits she gets from anxiety (yes, there are a few upsides)—she has a strong sense of empathy and sensitivity, which she uses to connect with and express the characters she portrays. You might also find the experience fun and gain the opportunity to meet new people who share your interest. Consider joining a local or community acting group, try a class at a local college, sign up for an improv event, or volunteer to help a local high school production.

Movies

I love going to the theater and getting lost in a movie. It is a place where my mind settles, and I can be completely engrossed. My worries from life and the outside world just turn off. There is nothing else seeking my attention. The big screen and surround sound are so absorbing. Although not quite the same, I also enjoy a TV series or documentary as an effective way to occupy my mind. I find it to be a great distraction, and I can do it alone or with family and friends. Nicole and I love to find an interesting Netflix series and immerse ourselves in it together for hours or even on occasion, days.

Read a Book

I love getting lost in a good book as much as watching a good movie. It gives me a distraction from my thoughts. Since you are reading this book, I am going to assume you already have this one in your coping tool kit! Thank you for taking the time to read our book. We hope it was informative and helpful. Read on!

Demystifying the Spectrum of Medical Treatments Available

Medication

What was your reaction when you read Emily's comment about her decision to start taking medication? Each one of us has a personal perspective on treatment options and the power to decide which ones are right for us. I believe taking medication for a mental-health condition is no different than taking medication for a physical condition. I take medication for cholesterol and anxiety every day. What is the difference? Scientific evidence and research have proven medication helps with mental-health conditions. Medication shaming is part of the stigma. Let it go.

Therapy

Finding and engaging with a qualified licensed therapist can be an effective way to treat anxiety. It can also honestly be hard to find the right one…the one you connect with who gets you. If it doesn't happen out of the gate, don't give up. Keep searching. It will be worth it. If you tried one and it wasn't a match, don't assume therapy isn't for you. It is a bit like dating. You will know when it is right.

It worked for Jackie, Rachel, James, and others. Each of us must find our own combination of treatments that work specifically for us. If you decide to see a therapist, I recommend you consider cognitive behavior therapy. It is based on research and outcome data, which is available online. Go ahead, Google it and see what it has to offer.

Cognitive behavior therapy is based on the premise that what we feel is determined by what we think. By exploring beliefs and thoughts about past events, your thoughts can be altered and emotional reactions to past inaccurate or misperceptions about self-image, the past, and the world around you can be processed. CBT therapy can assist people in changing the way they think and give them the ability to improve thought patterns and create more positive self-talk. Psychotherapy helps you stop self-destructive thoughts and discover ways to change behaviors. Your inner dialogue can become more positive as you learn techniques to confront and control your anxiety.

Therapy has the potential to help you realize negative events may have been overly or inaccurately personalized, that perhaps your thinking is confined to black and white (dichotomous) thoughts, and/or focusing only on the negative is a choice. A cognitive behavior therapist guides you to confront misperceptions in your thinking. Once you see and acknowledge these, you can change your outlook, mood, and possibly your life. It helped Emily and Zack. It might be able to help you too. What do you have to lose?

Motherly Advice

While writing this book in collaboration with Nicole, I had the opportunity to reflect about my life, decisions, choices, and future. I recalled my childhood and raising my kids. I gained a renewed appreciation for my friends and family who embraced our project and message for our book. I am grateful to everyone who volunteered and shared their inner thoughts and personal experiences. I feel blessed to be surrounded by a rich circle of supportive and loving family and friends.

My final revelation about my anxiety came as a surprise. My husband and I had been in marriage counseling for several months when it became clear to me the impact anxiety and mental illness was having on our family dynamics. In therapy, I discovered how anxiety has impacted our entire family. I didn't see it. But anxiety and depression actually had been in complete control of our family for years, maybe even decades.

Since the day my children were born, I have felt compelled to protect them from life's hardships. I did not identify it as anxiety, but there it was. My compulsion to protect my children from anger and rejection propelled me to put their every need first in my life. I could not tolerate them experiencing stress, pressure, demands, criticism, or pain.

When my children are upset, I am upset. Years ago, my boss offered me a perspective I have always remembered. She asked me to consider if my children did not experience anger, pain, and disappointment in childhood, how were they going to develop the tolerance or skills to handle adversity as adults? I have to admit there was wisdom in those words. Both of my children are now living on their own. I can see they have the life skills they need. I know they can handle life independently because I see them doing it. They are forging their own path and building their own lives.

Although it clearly did not work, I did everything I could think of to build up my children's self-esteem as they were growing up. Right or wrong, at least now I understand my actions. Did I overprotect them? Probably. But no harm, no foul. They are stronger than I ever hoped they would be.

My final recommendation for your consideration is central to chipping away at the root of anxiety. Are you ready? Drum roll please. Here it is.

Love and accept yourself. Yep, it is that difficult and yet that simple.

Give yourself the same unconditional love you lavish on others. Seriously, why listen to your inner voice telling you that you are a failure, or not capable of something? It is clueless. When the negative voice rises up from within you, imagine you are talking to a friend struggling with these same doubts and thoughts. What advice would you give to comfort and reassure her? What words of support and empathy would you offer? There you go, take that advice.

Don't be your own worst enemy. There is no value in beating yourself up all day, every day. Life does a good enough job of that already. Free yourself a little at a time and treat yourself with respect. See the good; there is a great deal of good within you. Look until you see it. It is there. Work towards accepting who you are, including your flaws and anxiety. *You are wonderfully you. Embrace your uniqueness.* No one else on earth has the same thoughts and talents you do. Discover ways to be more of who you truly are and share that with the world. Use your inner voice for good.

Gaining insight is essential to getting help for your mental illness. If you are afraid and not willing to accept that you are someone who is mentally ill, it is a true barrier to seeking treatment. If you are at the turning point, it could be helpful to talk to someone who is comfortable living with their mental-health issues. Have a real conversation. I bet you will discover that you are not alone. Anxiety is simply a medical condition. It is not a reason or excuse for not living a fulfilled life. You wouldn't judge a friend who has emotional issues so don't judge yourself. Join us. Be a mental-health warrior. Raise awareness and decrease the discrimination and stigma.

That's all the mom advice I have to share today. By now, you understand my children are the most important people in my life. I intended to end by expressing a few final thoughts about them. But I find myself unable (even though I am officially an author) to find the words to describe what they mean to me.

There will never be any greater privilege than raising those two beautiful humans. Oh, wait a minute—according to Robyn, Liz, and Wendy, maybe being a grandmother tops it! I will have to get back to you on that one.

As an advocate, I see signs of hope for the future of mental health. There are distinct cracks forming in the stigma as public perceptions are shifting and people are sharing their stories. Lately, several high profile celebrities, athletes, and successful business executives have publicly shared their struggles with mental health. This helps.

Our culture is starting to understand we all have mental health just like we all have physical health. The brain is an organ and deserves as much respect and medical treatment as the heart or kidneys. This helps.

Mental health services are becoming more accessible and virtual medical and therapy appointments are making treatment more convenient. Brain research is on the rise. Psychiatry as a profession is gaining recognition for its role in overall health. This helps.

Colleges, universities, vocational institutions, and public and private school systems across the country are starting to understand the importance of investing in training their teachers, aides, and professors on mental-health warning signs and coping strategies so they in turn, can educate and support staff, students, and parents. By offering insight and training, people in these roles who have a responsibly for the care, education, and success of students can step in, make referrals, and offer help before it is too late. This helps.

All employers, but especially those who employ direct care workers, elder care workers, health care workers and child care workers, can improve the quality of their services, increase productivity, decrease employee absenteeism, improve employee retention, and attract new talent by building a strong culture of employee wellness which includes mental health. This helps.

I believe the most important and powerful way we eliminate the stigma of living with mental health is to change the perception and picture of what mental health looks like one person at a time… because it looks like all of us. It looks like the professional athlete, the celebrity, the executive, the teacher, the truck driver, the stock clerk, the maintenance employee, the policeman, your next door neighbor, your mother, your son, your plumber, your co-worker, your boss, your doctor, the waitress, the postal worker…it looks like me and probably you or someone you love. This helps.

Most of all please know that YOU ARE NOT ALONE, and it is okay to get the help you need or want. It is okay to talk about your fears, experiences, and your story. Be you with all you have. Be proud of your strength and resiliency. Show yourself and the world what you are made of. Yes, some days are harder than others, but you got this.

References

1.   American Psychiatric Association. *Diagnostic and Statistical Manual of Mental Disorders, 5th ed.*

2.   Craske, M.S., MB, *Anxiety.* Lancet, 2016. **388**: p. 3048-59.

3.   Kennard, B., et al., *Remission and residual symptoms after short-term treatment in the Treatment of Adolescents with Depression Study (TADS).* J Am Acad Child Adolesc Psychiatry, 2006. **45**(12): p. 1404-11.

4.   Beesdo-Baum, K. and S. Knappe, *Developmental epidemiology of anxiety disorders.* Child Adolesc Psychiatr Clin N Am, 2012. **21**(3): p. 457-78.

5.   Patton, G.C., C; Romaniuk, H; Mackinnon, A; Carlin, JB; Degenhardt, L; Olsson, CA; Moran, P *The prognosis of common mental disorders in adolescents: a 14-year prospective cohort study.* Lancet, 2014. **383**: p. 1404-11.

6.   Wilens, T., C. Zulauf, and J. Rosenbaum, *Psychiatric and Substance Use Disorders in Transitioning Adolescents and Young Adults*, in *Massachusetts General Hospital Comprehensive Clinical Psychiatry.* 2016, Elsevier: New York.

7.   Blanck, P., et al., *Effects of mindfulness exercises as stand-alone intervention on symptoms of anxiety and depression: Systematic review and meta-analysis.* Behavior Research and Therapy, 2018. **102**: p. 25 - 35.

8.   Calkins, A., et al., *Anxiety Disorders*, in *Massachusetts General Hospital Comprehensive Clinical Psychiatry*. 2016, Elsevier: New York. p. 353 - 366.

9.   Major, B. and L. O'Brien, *The Social Psychology of Stigma*. Annual Review of Psychology, 2005. **56**: p. 393 - 421.

10. Moncrieff, J., P. Byrne, and M. Crawford, *Challenges to psychiatry: Antipsychiatry, the user movement and stigma*, in *Core Psychiatry*. 2012, Elsevier. p. 155-164.

11. Johnson, R.J., R.J. Turner, and B. Link, *Sociology of Mental Health*. 2014: Springer International Publishing.

12. Link, B. and J. Phelan, *Conceptualizing Stigma*. Annual Review of Sociology, 2001. **27**: p. 365 -383.

About the Authors

Lori Maney Lentini, M.S. is a respected mental-health advocate who lives with an anxiety disorder and works as a Senior Vice President at a large not-for-profit agency in New York, which serves over 14,000 people a year with mental health, developmental disabilities, and substance abuse disorders.

Her experience in the mental-health field as an executive, patient, and parent of grown children with mental-health issues culminate into a richly honest and authentic voice with universal appeal. These experiences are the foundation from which she delivers a message of hope, understanding, and real-life strategies for coping with stress and anxiety. As an executive leader and member of the Leadership Council with 26 years of service, Lori has collaborated on and led the organization's expansion from a $5 million organization to a $100 million+ organization today. This strategic growth has significantly increased the size, scope, diversity, and geographical reach of services available in the community.

In 2019, Lori was appointed to serve in the role as the Peer Advocate on the Agency's Incident Review Committee, which oversees the quality of care patience receive to ensure the voice and perspective of someone living with a mental illness is present to advocate for service improvements and fair treatment. She is also a member of the Orange County Chamber of Commerce Health & Wellness Committee, a collaborative of employers working together with the county to improve the mental and physical wellness of employees through implementing innovative employer practices, policies, and public education.

Lori is a sought-after corporate leadership trainer specializing in professional development, coaching, and culture transformation. Her seminars have focused on staff emotional wellbeing, cultural diversity, joy at work, team building, managing multi-generational teams, leave policies, and supporting people with illness and disabilities at work, positive culture design, and staff retention. She has a master's degree in Human Resources Management and Counseling and is trained in Mental Health First Aid and Suicide Prevention: Question Persuade Refer (QPR). She is a trainer for A Hero's Journey workshop and is currently seeking certification as a Mental Health First Aid trainer.

In her journey supporting family, friends, co-workers, and staff, she has reaffirmed the importance backed by research and federal initiatives for people of all abilities to have the opportunity for employment as a significant social determent of health. Overcoming isolation, loneliness, and finding employment are among the biggest barriers for people with disabilities and are essential to their physical and mental health, leading to more productive and happy lives. Lori is committed to ensuring that all people have access to training, support, and fulfilling opportunities for work. She has chaired business initiatives in the community to employ people with significant mental health and developmental disabilities, resulting in thousands of disabled people gaining competitive employment. She is a deeply devoted and loving mother of two, her daughter, Nicole and son, James.

Dr. Nicole Lentini is a resident Physician in Psychiatry Northwestern Hospital in Chicago. She has personally struggled with both anxiety and depression and is now completing advanced training to help others struggling with severe mental illness. She has conducted research in several areas of psychology and psychiatry including the effects of chronic stigma on those with mental illness as well as research dedicated to finding the best ways medical teams can support patients and families during very stressful times such as ICU admissions. She has chosen to share her journey with mental illness in an attempt to lessen the stigma about what those living with mental illness look like and are capable of achieving with treatment and support. By adding her story to this collection and sharing the insight she has gained professionally and personally, she is intent on altering the perception of how people view mental illness.